Alexander Paul

The History of Reform

A Record of the Struggle for the Representation of the People in Parliament

Alexander Paul

The History of Reform
A Record of the Struggle for the Representation of the People in Parliament

ISBN/EAN: 9783337151805

Printed in Europe, USA, Canada, Australia, Japan

Cover: Foto ©ninafisch / pixelio.de

More available books at **www.hansebooks.com**

THE
HISTORY OF REFORM

A RECORD OF THE STRUGGLE

FOR THE

REPRESENTATION OF THE PEOPLE IN PARLIAMENT

By ALEXANDER PAUL

AUTHOR OF "SHORT PARLIAMENTS"

LONDON

GEORGE ROUTLEDGE AND SONS

BROADWAY, LUDGATE HILL

NEW YORK: 9 LAFAYETTE PLACE

1884

LONDON:
BRADBURY, AGNEW, & CO., PRINTERS, WHITEFRIARS.

CONTENTS.

———◆———

CHAPTER I.

EARLY DEMANDS FOR REFORM.

CHAPTER II.

THE FIRST REFORM BILLS.

CHAPTER III.

PITT'S REFORM BILL.

CHAPTER IV.

FLOOD'S HOUSEHOLD SUFFRAGE BILL.

CHAPTER V.

REFORM SOCIETIES. PERSECUTION OF REFORMERS.

CHAPTER VI.

LEADING UP TO 1831.

CHAPTER X.

MR. GLADSTONE'S REFORM BILL.

APPENDIX.

HISTORY OF REFORM.

CHAPTER I.

EARLY DEMANDS FOR REFORM.

AT what date does the story of Reform begin ? The period most vividly associated with the word Reform in the mind of the modern politician is little more than half a century past ; but the great struggle which culminated in the Act of 1832 had its real beginnings at a much earlier date. It will soon be a century and a half since the demand for Parliamentary Reform —in the sense of an extension of the electorate—first took shape. We are already within six years of a century since the time when it was proposed by Henry Flood that members of Parliament should be returned by the resident

11

householders in every county. And more than a hundred years ago the schemes of universal suffrage now advocated by our most extreme Reformers were placed before the Parliament and the country. A date is wanted which while offering a suitable starting point on the path of Reform, will not take us so far on the road as to leave us a confused retrospect. Such a convenient date is 1745.

The year chosen will be recognized as that of the Scotch rebellion. The events of the time obliged George II. to convene Parliament at an earlier day than was anticipated, and upon the debate on the address, Sir Francis Dashwood brought in an amendment in favour of legisla-tion, "for securing to His Majesty's faithful subjects the perpetual enjoyment of their un-doubted right to be freely and fairly represented in Parliament." The disturbed state of Scot-land was an obvious and a successful plea for dismissing this amendment; but it was acknow-ledged by some who refused to support Sir F. Dashwood, that as soon as the rising should be put down, it would be well to support the liberties of the people against the fatal effects of corruption, which, said Sir J. Philips, were as much to be dreaded as any effects that could ensue from the success of the rebellion. This allusion by Sir J. Philips to corruption opens up our retrospect.

The corrupt state of Parliament had been so long notorious as to be the chief thought in the minds of the people whenever the pinch of the shoe of government was felt. Boroughs had been, and could be bought and sold, but Walpole had boasted that he found it easier to buy the members. The question with the Reformers before 1745, therefore, chiefly, was how to get the control of the members out of the hands of ministers, and into the hands of the constituencies. And this is why up to that time we hear, not of franchise extension, but of bills for preventing members being bribed with places and pensions, and of cries for a return to triennial Parliaments, which would give the country a chance of changing their members if they ceased to be representative. Short parliaments had been once wrung with great difficulty from William III., as a remedy against Parliamentary corruption, from which the nation had already suffered since the Restoration. Unfortunately, the Parliament that was sitting in 1716, considered it proper·and necessary to extend its own duration to secure the new dynasty, and the Parliaments were thenceforth elected for seven years. In Sir Francis Dashwood's day, it had begun at last to dawn upon the nation that some more extensive reform was necessary, for in the face of growing scandals as to the nature of some of the constituencies, there was no security that members of Parliament even when frequently elected, would be the representatives of the people rather than the tools of ministers.

In the next quarter of a century (after 1745), there was nothing done by way of amendment, a bribery Act of 1762 failing to touch the case of the boroughmongers ; and we may judge of the growth of the scandal by the statement in

one of Chesterfield's letters, that he offered
£2,500 for a secure seat in Parliament, and was
laughed at.   The borough-jobber said there was
no such thing as a borough to be had then.
The rich East and West Indians had secured
them at the rate of £3,000 at least, but many at
£4,000, and two or three that he knew at
£5,000.   Chesterfield expressed surprise that in
1768 the Northampton election had cost the
contending parties at least £30,000 a side, and
that a borough had been sold to two members
for £9,000.   Burke complained of public money
shamefully squandered, of millions misapplied
to the purposes of venality and corruption.
Chatham described corruption as the great
original cause of the discontents of the people
themselves, of the enterprise of the Crown, and
the injurious decay of the internal vigour of the
constitution.   The borough of Gatton was sold
for the enormous sum of £75,000.   While, by
the development of such scandals, the public
mind was being fully prepared for reform, the
dispute with America arose, and Parliament re-

fused to let Wilkes take his seat for Middlesex. The stirring events of the day led to inquiry into ancient popular rights, and gave birth to projects of reform far in advance of those which had occurred to the previous generation.

The retrospect was now extended. The far-off times, when sturdy freemen refused to be taxed without their consent given in Parliament, and when it was an axiom of the constitution that what concerned all should be approved by all, were brought prominently under notice. Inquiry was made into the early state of the representation, and history told this tale. From the time when Parliament had assumed its permanent structure, sovereigns had recognised that parliaments existed for redress, "not only in matters of law, but in grievances against the king's ministers." It had been conceded that these parliaments should be held frequently, and that they should be elected "openly and indifferently," the members being two knights from every shire, and two citizens from every city, and two burgesses from every borough in the sheriff's jurisdiction. There was no doubt that the freemen had then paid wages to Members of Parliament. The duty had, unfortunately, been deemed a burden at the time. But the electors were less devoted to their duties than they might have been could they have seen what consequences to posterity would have resulted from their neglect. But a Parliamentary history, not long published, told how on one occasion, when King Richard II.'s Council sought to influence an election in his Majesty's favour, the sheriffs made reply that " it would be almost impossible to oppose any person against the people's liking, for they would easily guess at the design and stand the more resolutely upon their right." When it was not the king, but the sheriff who abused his position, either to favour constituencies who wished to be saved expense, or to gratify some motive of his own, the parliament made strict laws to provide against such abuses ; and also enacted that both electors and elected should be resident. But the most striking proof of the wide

extent of the ancient electorate was found in
the Act of Parliament which brought into prominence in our constitution the forty-shilling
freeholder. This has since been rightly called
by the historians a great disfranchising Act. It
first declared that, " a very great and excessive
number of people, for the most part of small
substance and no value, pretended a voice in
the elections equivalent with the most worthy
knights and esquires dwelling within the same
counties." Then these worthy knights and
esquires, whose pride was so much shocked by
the electoral equality of their humbler brethren,
calmly proceeded, in that eighth year of Henry
VI.'s reign, to oust from their right of voting
all persons who had not free land or tenement
to what was then the considerable value of forty
shillings per annum. They did this, too, on a
rather mean pretence. Alleging no actual in-
competence on the part of the humbler voters,
but taking upon themselves the rôle of prophets
as well as legislators, they assumed that, unless
their act were passed, " manslaughters, riots,

batteries, and divisions among the gentlemen and people of the same counties," would "very likely arise and be." If in the counties there had thus been a deliberate disfranchisement of householders, the limitation of the popular vote in the boroughs had been effected by a quieter and more insidious process. Sometimes, out of compassion for the poor and insignificant boroughs, to whom the payment of members was burdensome, and sometimes for less disinterested motives, the sheriff had neglected to comply with the strict summons requiring him to return members from every city and borough. The fatal indifference of our forefathers to the electoral privileges which have since been so slowly regained, enabled the sheriffs to assume discretionary powers in regard to the return of members, until at length, in the same reign as the Forty-shilling Freeholders statute, they were required, under heavy penalties, to issue their precepts without fraud. This remedial statute had its unfortunate aspects. It fixed the franchise in boroughs even

after they had become ruined and decayed ; so
that it was in vain that James I. charged the
sheriffs " not to send their precepts for the electing or returning of any burgesses to or for any
antient borough towns within their counties
being so ruined and decayed that there were
not sufficient residents to make such choice, and
of whom lawful election might be made." The
king's command could not prevail over an Act
of Parliament. The boroughs were not to be
disfranchised by a royal edict. But royal
charters had been responsible for obscuring
ancient electoral privileges and rights. When
the Tudors and the Stuarts wanted money aids,
they gave to boroughs charters containing important rights. To the community these rights
were of so much consequence that they were
blinded to the significance of those political
arrangements by which the right of returning a
member was in many cases vested in a limited
body, instead of the inhabitants paying "scot
and lot."* The boroughs had thus become

* Canon Stubbs (now Bishop of Chester), in his " Con-

easily open to manipulation ; and now, even some fifty years before they were finally dealt with in the Reform Bill of 1832, houseless Old Sarum, and Gatton with its half-dozen buildings, were by-words in Parliament.

"What a happy fate," said Wilkes, one day, in Parliament, "has attended the boroughs of Gatton and Old Sarum, of which, although *ipsæ periére ruinæ*, the names are familiar to us, the clerk regularly calls them over and four respectable gentlemen represent their departed greatness, as the knights at a coronation represent Aquitaine and Normandy." Recalling the largest division he could recollect, Wilkes showed that, notwithstanding the population of England was some five millions, 254 English members were the representatives of but 5723 persons, mostly the inhabitants of Cornish and other insignificant

stitutional History," says :—" The newer the constitution of the town was, the less liberal the constitution seems to have been, and several places which must in early times have enjoyed fairly free institutions, had, by accepting new charters, lost their liberties, at all events in this particular (the right of voting)."

boroughs, while there were 56 members in the House elected by only 364 persons. The great towns were unrepresented. There had been no acknowledgment of their growth and importance except for a brief time in the days of the Commonwealth.

The rotten boroughs served one good purpose. With some of them, where population remained, there had survived the ancient franchise, and Reformers ever since have seized upon the fact, that, in many of these boroughs, the franchise was vested in the freemen, in the inhabitants paying scot and lot, or in the resident house-holders generally. It was to all these facts that, in the latter half of the last century, men began to direct their attention, and to resolve that a mere reversion to short Parliaments would not cure the disease of the constitution. Parliament they found must not only be re-elected often, but it must be made more representative when it was elected.

The note, therefore, sounded by Sir. F. Dash-wood in 1745 was taken up as the keynote of a

great agitation with this view. A society called
the "Supporters of the Bill of Rights" sprang
into existence in 1769, with the view of eliciting
pledges from candidates for Parliamentary
election. They were the first active body of
Reformers. They required every candidate to
aim at a full and equal representation of the
people in Parliament, at annual Parliaments, at
exclusion of place-holders from Parliament, at
the impeachment of ministers who had violated
the rights of the Middlesex electors, at the
acknowledgment of America's right of self-
taxation, and at satisfaction of Irish grievances.

Chatham in 1770 saw the agitation that was
brewing, and tried to stave off what he regarded
as violent expedients. He admitted the corruption of the boroughs. He adopted the description of them as the rotten parts of the constitution. He had lived, he said, in Cornwall, and
had seen enough to justify the appellation. But
in his judgment they were to be treated as a
natural infirmity of the constitution, and, instead
of lopping off the rotten branches, he proposed

to "infuse new health into the constitution," by the addition of one extra representative for each of the counties. The proposition was unheeded, as it also was in 1771, when Chatham told the Earl of Buchan that a plan for more equal re-presentation by additional knights of the shire, seemed "highly seasonable." In 1774 it was still possible for Burke, as it was long to con-tinue possible for others, to speak, in the House of Commons, of "these walls of corruption." The neglect of the Reform question in Parlia-ment strengthened the agitation without, and the two Reform Bills first introduced to the notice of the Houses of Parliament were plans of universal suffrage.

CHAPTER II.

THE FIRST REFORM BILLS.

THERE is little danger, it may be assumed, of wearying a present-day reader with somewhat extended details of the first * propositions for franchise extension put before Parliament, after the time of Cromwell. These proposals were based on the principle of universal suffrage. The arguments in their favour are as interesting to-day as at the time they were first used ; and at a time when the enfranchisement of nearly every "capable citizen," is contemplated by the

* There was one previous Reform Bill in 1668, but it proceeded on the plan of increasing the knights of the shire as afterwards suggested by Chatham, rather than on an increase of representatives. It, however, proposed that some of the small boroughs, where there were but few electors, might be taken away. The author of the bill was Sir Thomas Meres. His proposal was rejected by 65 to 50.

government, as the object of an extended household and lodger franchise, it can hardly fail to be
of special interest to note the reasons urged in
Parliament for a still wider franchise in the
years 1776 and 1780.

John Wilkes was the author of the scheme of
1776. A just and equal representation of the
people of England in Parliament was its object,
and thenceforward a just and equal representation was long a popular out-door cry. The scope
of the proposed measure was wide. It provided
for enfranchisement; it proposed disfranchisement. Depopulated towns and boroughs should
no longer send members. The scheme was
felicitously described in classical phrase, Inutiles
ramos amputans ; feliciores inserit. " Every free
agent in the kingdom " was to be represented in
Parliament. Electors of the rotten boroughs were
to vote in the counties. London, and the more
populous counties, were to have an increased
representation. The great provincial towns also,
such as Birmingham, Manchester, Sheffield,
Leeds and others, were to send representatives

to the council of the nation. The proposal was a sweeping one to be made in that day, when the London representatives were elected only by liverymen, when leaseholders and copyholders in the country had no vote, and when Scotland's forty-five representatives were regarded as representing only themselves. It was thus justified by Wilkes :—

" I wish, sir, an English Parliament to speak the free unbiassed sense of the body of the English people, of every man among us, of each individual who may justly be supposed to be comprehended in a fair majority. The meanest mechanic, the poorest peasant and day-labourer has important rights respecting his personal liberty, that of his wife and children, his property, however inconsiderable, his wages, his earnings, the very price and value of each day's hard labour which are in many trades and manufactures regulated by the power of Parliament. Every law relative to marriage, to the protection of a wife sister or daughter against violence and brutal lust, to every contract or agreement with a rapacious or unjust master, is of importance to

c

the manufacturer; the cottager, the servant as well as to the rich subjects of the State. Some share therefore in the power of making those laws which deeply interest them, and to which they are expected to pay obedience, should be reserved even to this inferior, but most useful set of men in the community. We ought always to remember this important truth, acknowledged by every free state, that all government is instituted for the good of the mass of the people to be governed ; that they are the original fountain of power, and even of revenue, and in all events the last resource."

Leave was not given to Wilkes to introduce his bill, but the speech from which the above is an extract, stands in Parliamentary history as a mark to indicate the beginning of a movement for what was subsequently known as Radical Reform.

Out of doors the idea of universal suffrage had already exercised a fascinating influence upon the public mind. Major Cartwright, one of the most celebrated pioneers of Reform, had vigorously advocated annual Parliaments, universal suffrage, and the ballot in 1774, in a work entitled "Take your Choice; or the Legislative Rights of the Commonalty Vindicated;" and "One man, one vote," a cry which may have had a novel sound to some in 1883 was one of Cartwright's political principles. There were differences of opinion among his adherents on the question of the ballot, but the proposition for short Parliaments and universal suffrage appealed not only to the populace. Several men of standing and culture declared their concurrence in his views. The learned Sir William Jones was in accord with these advanced political opinions. So were several noblemen, among whom was conspicuous the Duke of Richmond, the author of the next Universal Suffrage Bill. To explain the state of public feeling which made such proposals in Parliament even possible at this early date, it should be stated that at the end of 1779 a great meeting of the clergy and freeholders of the county of York had been held to complain of the enormous war expenditure, of the growing load of debt and taxes, and of the squandering of public money on sinecure places and on pensions. A Corresponding Committee had been formed to open communications with other counties, and for the next few months meetings to form new Corresponding Committees and to pass resolutions on the subject of a Reform in Parliament were being held all over the country. They did not confine their attention to economical reform, but pitched upon the necessity of an alteration of the Parliamentary system as the only cure of national grievances. The great topics of discussion were whether demands should be made upon Parliament for annual elections or for triennial elections, for a system of equal representation or for the addition to Parliament, as Chatham had proposed, of a hundred knights of the shire. The most prominent public men had to take up sides in the movement. Lord Shelburne wrote to the Devizes meeting in March, 1780, vindicating " the clear inalienable and indefeasible right of the people both to shorten the duration of Parliament and to equalise the representation," although at the same time he hinted the desirability of the people being content with moderate measures. The strength of the public feeling enabled Dunning to carry the celebrated motion declaring "that the power of the crown has increased, is increasing, and ought to be diminished."

In the early part of this year (1780) Cartwright's principles were greatly advanced by a society of his own founding called the Society for promoting Constitutional Information, which was joined by members of both Houses. By this Society was published the following curious and interesting document which is reproduced with its italics and capitals as found in a collection of their papers :—

DECLARATION
OF THOSE
Rights of the Commonalty of Great Britain
Without which they cannot be FREE.

IT IS DECLARED,

FIRST. That the government of this realm, and the making of laws for the same, ought to be lodged in the hands of King, Lords of Parliament, and Representatives of the *whole body* of the freemen of this realm.

2dly. That *every man* of the commonalty (excepting infants, insane persons, and criminals) is of common right, and by the laws of God, *a Freeman*, and entitled to the full enjoyment of *Liberty*.

3dly. That liberty or freedom consists in having an actual share in the appointing of those who frame the laws and who are to be the guardians of every man's life, property and peace : for the ALL of one man is as dear to him as the ALL of another ; and the poor man has an *equal* right, but *more* need to have representatives in the legislature than the rich one.

4thly. That they who have *no* voice nor vote in the electing of representatives *do not enjoy* liberty, but are absolutely *enslaved* to those who *have* votes, and to their representatives : for to be enslaved, is to have governors whom *other men have set over us*, and to be subject to laws *made by the representatives of others*, without having had representatives of our own to give consent in *our* behalf.

5thly. That *a very great majority* of the commonalty of this realm are denied the privilege of voting for representatives in Parliament ; and consequently, they are enslaved to *a small number*, who do now enjoy this privilege exclusively to themselves ; but who, it may be presumed, are far from wishing to continue in the exclusive possession of a privilege, by which their fellow-subjects are deprived of *common right*, of *justice*, of *liberty*, and which, if not communicated to ALL must speedily cause *the certain overthrow of our happy constitution* and enslave us ALL. And,

6thly and lastly. We also say and do assert that it is *the right* of the commonalty of this realm to elect a new House of Commons once in *every year*, according to ancient and sacred laws of the land : because, whenever a Parliament continues in being for a *longer term*, very great numbers of the commonalty, who have arrived at the years of manhood since the last election, and *therefore* have a right to be actually represented in the House of Commons, are then *unjustly deprived* of that right ; and because it has been found by experience that longer Parliaments are extremely liable to corruption and undue influence, and to become more dependent upon the crown than upon their constituents ; by which means the balance of the constitution is destroyed and the people's interests betrayed by those who are chosen to protect them.

When the above Declaration is compared with the present long parliaments and unequal representation of the people, which has brought this kingdom to the brink of ruin, every true friend to his country is solemnly called upon to use his utmost endeavours for the restoration of annual parliaments, and that right of voting, which God and the Constitution have given him. In his hearty labours to obtain these civil and just rights, let everyone practise the Christian rule, to do unto others as we would they should do unto us. Then will that blessed æra come, when every man shall be free and happy under his vine, on earth peace, and consequently glory to God in the highest.

A REAL FRIEND TO THE PEOPLE.

Entirely in accordance with the ideas set forth in the above document was the measure which Charles Lennox, the third Duke of Richmond, presented to the House of Lords on the 3rd of June, 1780. This measure is historically of the more importance because of the position of its framer, who served the Crown in several high capacities, and was a member of subsequent administrations. Fox, who did not subscribe to his scheme of reform, admitted at a later date that he looked upon the Duke as the most able and fitting man in the country to bring about a reform.

The bill was entitled "An Act for declaring and restoring the natural, inalienable, and equal right of all the Commons of Great Britain (infants, persons of insane mind, and criminals incapacitated by law, alone excepted) to vote in the election of their representatives in Parliament, for regulating the mode and manner of such elections, for restoring annual Parliaments, for giving an hereditary seat to the sixteen peers which shall be elected for Scotland, and for establishing more equitable regulations concerning the peerage of Scotland." The whole measure would take up too much space in this small book, but the following is the part referring to suffrage extension in the preamble to the enacting clauses to be presently in brief explained :—

"Whereas the life, liberty, and property of every man is or may be affected by the law of the land in which he lives, and every man is bound to pay obedience to the same; and whereas by the constitution of this kingdom the right of making laws is vested in three estates, of King, Lords, and Commons in parliament assembled, and the consent of all the three said estates, comprehending the whole community, is

necessary to make laws which bind the whole
community; and whereas the House of Commons
represents all the commons of the realm, and
the consent of the House of Commons binds
the consent of all the commons of the realm in
cases in which the legislature is competent to
decide; and whereas no man is or can be
actually represented who hath not a vote in the
election of his representative; and whereas it is
the right of every commoner in this realm
(infants, persons of insane mind, and criminals
incapacitated by law, only excepted) to have a
vote in the election of the representative who is
to give his consent to the making of laws by
which he is to be bound; and whereas the
number of persons who are suffered to vote for
the election of members of the House of Commons do not at this time amount to one-sixth
part of the whole commons of this realm,
whereby far the greater part of the said
commons are deprived of their right to elect
their representatives, and the consent of the
majority of the whole community is given
by persons whom they have not delegated
for such purpose, and the majority of the
said community are governed by laws made by

a very small part of the said community, and to which the said community has not in fact consented by themselves or by their representatives; and whereas the state of election of members of the House of Commons hath, in process of time, so grossly deviated from its simple and natural principle of representation and equality that in several places members are returned by the property of *one man*, that the smallest boroughs send as many members as the largest counties, and that the majority of the representatives of the whole nation are chosen by a number of voters not exceeding 12,000; now for remedy of such partial and unequal representation, and of the many mischiefs which have arisen therefrom, be it declared and enacted," &c.

Those provisions of the bill with which this narrative is concerned were to this effect: Every man not disqualified in the manner referred to in the preamble was to have a vote. The number of members of the House of Commons (then 558) was to remain unaltered. Means were to be taken to discover the precise number

who were entitled to the new franchise. The
total was to be divided by 558, and the quotient
to be deemed the proportion of voters entitled
to elect one member at the first election under
the new system. The country was to be divided
into districts containing as nearly as possible
the 558th part of the total number of voters.
These districts were to be the future parliamentary boroughs of the kingdom. In each of
these districts a proclamation was to be made
in the middle of May every year inviting candidates for the next new parliament, to be
elected on the 1st September following. The
names of all candidates who offered themselves within a month were to be made public
before the 17th of June, at which date the inhabitants at an open meeting were to consider
the candidature of these persons and to declare
in favour of any others. All names submitted
in writing that day to the returning officer with
the sanction of the signatures of at least one
hundred inhabitants, were to be forwarded to
the Secretary of State as the list of candidates

for the borough.   By him these names were to
be published in the, *Gazette*; and thereafter no
one else might become a candidate.   The poll
was to be taken in the borough on the 1st
September, and each voter was to be bound to
take oath that he was a natural-born subject of
Great Britain, that he was 21 years of age, that
he had not during the day voted already in that
or any other parish, and that he was not an
officer, non-commissioned officer, warrant officer,
drummer or private man in the embodied
militia, navy or army.   It must not be inferred
from this last requirement that the men
engaged in the services were to be deprived of
the right of voting.   On the contrary, it was
declared to be unjust that men who exposed their
lives for the defence of their country should be
deprived of those "essential rights," which it
was proposed to restore to every subject.   But
the wisdom of making special provision for
them had often been demonstrated by incidents
at elections under the existing circumstances.
Whole regiments were put on the freemen's roll

of a particular borough just before the election, in order that they might be marched up to the polling booth when the proper time came to swamp the ordinary votes of the constituency. How much more readily could these tricks be played under a system of manhood suffrage? The Duke of Richmond's bill therefore proposed that those of our forces who were serving at home should certainly vote, provided that they voted only in their own parishes. The publication of the candidates' names in the *Gazette* so long before the election, made it possible to carry out this plan. If a soldier or sailor wished to vote, he was to go to a justice of the peace in the town where he happened to be, and give the place of his last settlement, so that his residence might be always certified to the proper officers in his own parish. On observing the names of his candidates in the *Gazette,* he could go at any time up to a certain date in August and give his vote as he chose for transmission by the justice of the peace, through the post, to the proper returning officer.

A more able advocacy of this plan than that which has been preserved to us in the record of the parliamentary proceedings of that time was given by the Duke in a celebrated letter which he wrote sometime afterwards to the commander of the Irish Volunteers. The following passages from the letter, considering the date on which they were written, cannot fail to be regarded as remarkable.

" The subject of Parliamentary Reform is that which, of all others, in my opinion, most deserves the attention of the public, as I conceive it would include every other advantage which the nation could wish. And I have no hesitation in saying that from every consideration which I have been able to give to this great question, that for many years has occupied my mind, and from every day's experience to the present hour, I am more and more convinced that the restoring the right of voting universally to every man not incapacitated by nature for want of reason or by law for the commission of crimes together with annual elections is the only Reform that can be effectual and permanent. I am further convinced that it is the only Reform that is practicable. * * * The second address of the Yorkshire committee to the people, confesses that our claims are founded on the true principles of the constitution, and only objects to them on the ground of impracticability. But their plan has now had a fair trial, and (if it is from the inclination of Parliament that practicability is to be expected) has been found as impracticable as ours. The more extensive plan, at the same time that its operation is more complete, depends on a more effectual support, that of the people. I am also persuaded that if the scheme for additional county members had proceeded any further, infinite difficulties would have arisen in adjusting it. * * * A few great families might divide a county between them, and choose the members by a house list like East-India directors. * * * But the greatest objection in my opinion to this and every other narrow and contracted plan of Reform, is that it proceeds upon the same bad principle as the abuse it pretends to rectify. *It is still partial and unequal.* The vast majority of the community is left unrepresented, and its most essential concerns, life, liberty, and pro-

perty, continue in the absolute disposal of those
whom they do not choose and over whom they
have no control. In the arrangement of plans
of this kind, there is no leading principle to
determine that the addition ought to be 100,
150, or 200, that the allotment should be according to population, property, or taxes paid in
each county, that any supposed proportion
between landed and trading interest is the
just one, and that the division of county
and city members will correspond with this
proportion when found. All is at sea without any compass to enable us to distinguish
the safe from the dangerous course : but in
the more liberal and great plan of *universal
representation* a clear and distinct principle at
once appears *that cannot lead us wrong* : not
conveniency but right. If it is not a maxim
of our constitution that a British subject is
to be governed only by laws to which he has
consented by himself or his representative, we
should instantly abandon the error, but if it is
the essential of freedom founded upon the
eternal principles of justice and wisdom, and our
unalienable birthright, we should not hesitate in
asserting it. Let us then but determine to act

upon this broad principle of giving TO EVERY MAN HIS OWN, and we shall immediately get rid of all the perplexities to which the narrow notions of partiality and exclusion must ever be subject. * * * It is true that the poorest man in the kingdom will have an equal vote with the first for the choice of the person to whom he trusts his all, and I think he ought to have that equal degree of security against oppression. It is also true that men of superior fortunes will have a superior degree of weight and influence, and I think that as education and knowledge generally attend property, those who possess them ought to have weight and influence with the more ignorant. But the essential difference will be, that although the people may be led they cannot be driven ; property will have its weight as it ever must have in all Governments, and I can see that in this plan it will precisely find its just proportion combined with talents and character. A man of great property that is beloved and esteemed, will, as he ought, have the greatest sway, but tyranny and oppression though attended with riches, may be resisted and will no longer be attended with a burgage tenure at command."

The Duke of Richmond did not omit to notice the argument with which even the more moderate reformers of the present day had to contend—the argument founded upon fear lest the admission of the lowest classes to the franchise should tend to the destruction of property. He maintained that the tendency would be the other way.   He said :—

"The equal rights of men to security from oppression, and to the enjoyment of love of liberty, strike me as perfectly compatible with their unequal shares of industry, labour, and genius, which are the origin of inequality of fortunes.   The equality and inequality of men are both founded in nature ; and whilst we do not confound the two, we cannot err. The protection of property appears to me one of the most essential ends of society ; and so far from injuring it by this plan, I conceive it to be the only means of preserving it, for the present system is hastening with great strides to a perfect equality in universal poverty."

No more brilliant exposition of the case of advocates of manhood suffrage could well be found than this ; and did space allow further quotation, it would be seen that this advanced Radical duke had more arguments to offer, even from a Conservative point of view ; for he was of opinion that Parliament, even in these days, was too much given to interfere with the executive, and he held that the executive power of governments might and would be left much more completely in their hands, provided that a broad suffrage and annual elections gave the people the power of speedily removing a government which was obviously using that power to the injury of the nation.

When Richmond introduced his Bill into Parliament, he described the boroughs as the very sink of corruption—dangerous to liberty, and a great engine in the hands of ministers to enforce measures contrary to the interests of the people. He mentioned, that in Lord Montague's park wall, he had seen several stones marked with numbers. These, on inquiry, he discovered to

represent votes for members of Parliament. He
stated that the clear majority of the House of
Commons was returned by not more than 6,000
men, while the right of voting for the whole of
England and Wales was confined to 210,000.
These anomalies, however, failed to help the
Duke of Richmond's legislative project ; and
any chance, indeed, that he might have had of
carrying his bill forward by a single stage was
lost, owing to the disturbed state of the metropolis at that moment by reason of the Gordon
riots.

It may not be unpleasing to the reader, while
it will certainly be appropriate to this stage of
the narrative if, by way of variety, this chapter
is concluded with the celebrated ode of Sir
William Jones, reflecting the spirit of the Reformers of that day. This ode, in which law,
based on popular will, is exalted in powerful
contrast with the government which depends
on the discretion of the few, was circulated
broadcast in 1781, by the Society for Constitutional Information, and its eloquent lines have

often done good service since, in the oratory
of Reformers.

> What constitutes a state ?
> Not high-raised battlement or labour'd mound,
>   Thick wall or moated gate ;
> Not cities proud with spires and turrets crown'd ;
>   Not bays and broad-arm'd ports,
> Where, laughing at the storm, rich navies ride ;
>   Not starr'd and spangled courts,
> Where low-brow'd baseness wafts perfume to pride ;
>   NO ! Men—high-minded men,
> With powers as far above dull brutes endued
>   In forest, brake, or den,
> As beasts excel cold rocks and brambles rude ;
>   Men, who their duties know,
> But know their rights, and knowing, dare maintain,
>   Prevent the long-aim'd blow,
> And crush the tyrant while they rend the chain :
>   These constitute a state,
> And sovereign Law, that state's collected will,
>   O'er thrones and globes elate
> Sits empress, crowning good, repressing ill ;
>   Smit by her sacred frown
> The fiend, Discretion, like a vapour, sinks,
>   And e'en th' all-dazzling Crown
> Hides his faint rays, and at her bidding shrinks.
>   Such was this heaven-lov'd isle,
> Than Lesbos fairer and the Cretan shore !
>   No more shall freedom smile ?
> Shall Britons languish, and be men no more ?

Since all must life resign,
Those sweet rewards, which decorate the brave,
'Tis folly to decline,
And steal inglorious to the silent grave.

CHAPTER III.

PITT'S REFORM BILL.

PITT brought forward, in Parliament, on several occasions, the subject of Reform, but had the misfortune, in the end, to incur the odium of all reformers, excepting perhaps, the Duke of Richmond, who, like himself, slackened in his zeal when he had been for some time a minister, so that, by the Radicals of their day, they were both together branded as apostates. The first effort made by Pitt to improve the representation was in 1782, when the hated ministry of Lord North had just been overthrown, and the Marquis of Rockingham became the head of a government in which places were held by the ducal author of the radical Reform Bill just described in the last chapter, and by Lord Ashburton, who as Mr. Dunning, had carried the famous motion in favour of diminishing the influence of the Crown. Pitt declaring himself confident in the new ministers, moved on the 7th of May for a committee to enquire into and report on the best means of carrying into execution "a moderate and substantial reform of the representation." He, like previous reformers, dwelt on the scandals of the boroughs. Some of these were governed, and others possessed by the Treasury; some returned members to the House without having any actual existence in property, population, trade or weight; others were so corrupt that they belonged, he said, more to the Nabob of Arcot than to the people of Great Britain.

Fox, in the course of this debate, complained that while Middlesex had an eighth part of the whole number of electors, paid a sixth part of the land-tax and a third of all other taxes, it had not more than a fifty-fifth part of the representation. He and several other distinguished men, such as Sir George Savile and the Earl of

Surrey, supported Pitt's motion, but on a division it was negatived by 161 votes to 141.

Pitt took office under Shelburne later in the same year, and when on the 6th May, 1783, he again made a proposition with regard to Reform it was disappointingly inadequate in the view of the more ardent reformers. He proceeded by way of a series of resolutions by which the House was to assent to the principle of disfranchising boroughs when the voters were convicted of gross corruption, and of giving new members to the counties and the metropolis. One of the most striking anomalies brought out on the discussion of these resolutions, was the fact that the Tower Hamlets, paying £34,000 a year land-tax, was unrepresented, while the County of Cornwall, paying £20,000 less, had actually only forty-two members. Lord North opposed these resolutions, and with characteristic coolness referred to his own downfall as the strongest proof that could be given of the potent efficacy of the public voice. Fox, and other supporters of Pitt's propositions, only regretted that he had not taken more efficient action, and a long debate resulted in the defeat of the resolutions by 243 to 149.

Attention having been directed to the proposals with regard to universal suffrage, it is desirable to note also that Pitt on this occasion discussed the expedient of giving "an indiscriminate franchise to all inhabitants as a right without which they could not be free," only to "condemn and utterly reject it." He used this ingenious argument :—

"If this doctrine should obtain, nearly one half of the people must in fact be slaves, for it is absolutely impossible that this idea of giving to every man a right of voting, however finely it may appear in theory, can ever be reduced to practice : but though it were even practicable, still one half of the nation would be slaves, for all those who voted for the unsuccessful candidates cannot in the strictness of this doctrine be said to be represented in Parliament, and therefore they are governed by laws to which they give not their assent, either in person or by representatives, consequently according to the ideas of the friends of this expedient, all those who vote for unsuccessful candidates must be slaves, nay it is often-times still harder, that those who are members of Parliament, are made slaves also, and are governed by laws to which they have not only not given their consent but against which they have actually voted. For my part, my idea of representation is this, that the members once chosen and returned to Parliament, are in fact the representatives of the people at large, as well of those who do not vote at all, or who, having voted, gave their votes against them, as of those by whose suffrages they were actually seated in the House. This being therefore my principle I cannot consent to an innovation founded on doctrines subversive of liberty, which in reality go so far as to say that this House of Commons is not, and that no House of Commons ever has been, a true and constitutional representation of the people, for no House of Commons has yet been elected by all the men in the kingdom."

On Pitt being made Prime Minister in the new ministry of December, 1783, great expectations were rife among the reformers as to what would now be done for them, and some disappointment was expressed that when an important reform petition came up from York, he took no more active measure in favour of a change in the law than that of expressing friendly sentiments in regard to the receipt of this document. Fox taunted Pitt on the subject of his selection of Ministers, of whom scarcely one was likely to support a Reform Bill. Pitt was afterwards stung to the quick by the reproaches of Alderman Sawbridge, who, in moving for a committee, in March, 1784, to enquire into the representation, gave voice to an apprehension that the Minister had abandoned all idea of Reform in his heart. The City, Westminster, Southwark, and the Counties of Middlesex and Surrey were now banded in a quintuple alliance for the purpose of securing Parliamentary Reform. It was not desirable in the Minister's interest that the feeling out of doors as to his lukewarmness should be encouraged. He hotly denounced the charges

of the alderman as "the most invidious, the
most false, the most malicious, and the most
slanderous." The violence of his language
in fact, brought upon him, the reproof of the
Speaker. Though Pitt returned to power
after a dissolution in May of this year, he found
it necessary to give a distinct pledge to bring
forward the subject of Parliamentary Reform,
upon which, on the testimony of Fox, the
people of the country were now "deeply, seriously, and universally interested." Burke as an
anti-reformer had such a clamour raised against
him in the House on the occasion of this pledge
being given, that he had to sit down without
being heard.

At length, on the 18th of April, 1785, Pitt's
historical scheme was brought forward. It was a
scheme intended to be "complete and final."
It was based nominally—advanced reformers
would not admit that it was based actually—
on the principle now laid down on ministerial authority that the House of Commons
ought to be "an assembly freely elected, be-

tween whom and the mass of the people, there was the closest union and most perfect sympathy."

The features of this Reform Bill may be thus set out :—

1. The electoral privileges of thirty-six rotten boroughs to be bought off.

2. The seventy-two members thus obtained to be distributed between the metropolis and the counties.

3. Copyholders in the counties to participate in the electoral rights hitherto confined to freeholders.

4. Borough corporations possessing right of election to be at liberty to make application to Parliament to surrender their exclusive privileges into the hands of the inhabitant householders occupying houses assessed to a certain small amount.

5. Other boroughs in addition to the thirty-six explicitly pointed out to be at liberty, as they fell into decay, to surrender their voting power, with a view to its transference to such

populous and flourishing towns, as might petition for representation in Parliament.

To the above scheme the main objections were to its purchase proposals, and to its gradual operation. A million of money was to be set apart in thirty-six shares, which were to accumulate interest until the sum became altogether irresistible to the borough each was destined to buy. It was only when all these thirty-six boroughs were bought up in this gradual manner, that operations were to be extended so as to bring the large cities into the representation, and then this could only be done by laying out another large sum of money for the purpose. A warm protest was lodged against this intended traffic in electoral privileges. Fox, as an ardent reformer, could not consent to purchase from a minority of electors, what he contended was the property of the whole people. Indeed, he would not allow that there was any property in the vote at all. A trust had been given the boroughs for constitutional purposes, and the nation had a right to resume possession of it.

E

Even Burke, who had little real sympathy with Reformers, and came by-and-by to show down-right hostility towards them, sarcastically asked whether the proprietors of the boroughs had not already been sufficiently well paid in the profusion of honours which had been always at their command in return for their political influence. It will be seen, however, that the Reformers had gained much by these propositions. The plan of the minister recognised the desirability of enfranchising copyholders in counties, and house-holders in towns, and it gave partial approval to the principle of representation of numbers. "It was the clear and determined opinion of every speculatist," said Pitt, "that there should be an alteration of the present proportion between the counties and boroughs, and that in that change a larger proportion of members should be given for the populous places than for places that had neither property nor people. * * He would take the criterion from which he should judge what boroughs were decayed from the number of houses, and this was a mode of judgment which was not liable to error and which he conceived to be perfectly consistent with the original principle of representation." The following passage from this speech has a permanent interest, and may be quoted also as an example of the great Statesman's elegant diction :—

" In times of calamity and distress how truly important is it to the people of this country that the House of Commons should sympathize with themselves, and that their interests should be indissoluble. It is most material that the people should have confidence in their own branch of the legislature. The force of the constitution as well as its beauty depends on that confidence and on the union and sympathy which exists between the constituent, and the representative. The source of our glory and the muscles of our strength are the pure character of freedom which our constitution bears. To lessen that character, to taint it is to take from our vitals a part of our vigour and to lessen not only our importance but our energy with our neighbours.

If we look back to our history, we shall find that
the brightest periods of its glory and its triumph
are those in which the country had the most
complete confidence in the House of Commons. The purity of the representation is the
only true and permanent source of such confidence, for though occasionally bright characters
have arisen who, in spite of the general corruption and depravity of the day in which they
lived manifested the superior influence of
integrity and virtue and forced both Parliament
and people to countenance their administration'
yet it would be unwise for the people of England
to leave their fate to the chance of such characters often arising, when prudence must dictate
that the certain way of securing their properties
and freedom is to purify the source of representation and to establish that strict relation
between themselves and the House of Commons, which it is the original idea of the constitution to create."

Pitt's plan of reform was intended to work
automatically, and to keep the representation

always distributed in such a manner that property and people would be together represented. Its ultimate extension of the electorate could not be foreseen, but it was calculated at the moment that it could be no long time before at least forty boroughs would submit to disfranchisement, while it was anticipated that ten corporations would forthwith surrender their exclusive right of representation. It was thus computed that the bill would speedily add to the electorate 99,000 new voters. But the motion for leave to bring in the bill, "after much extraneous debate and much personal allusion and animosities from both sides of the House," was negatived by 248 votes to 174.

CHAPTER IV.

FLOOD'S HOUSEHOLD SUFFRAGE BILL.

A MODIFIED household suffrage as appears from the last chapter, entered to a limited extent into the plan of Pitt. The first purely Household Suffrage Bill introduced to Parliament was brought forward by Henry Flood in the year 1790. He proposed simply that there should be 100 members elected by the resident householders in the counties. He estimated that the effect of his proposal would be to add 400,000 responsible citizens to the electorate. The sheriff of each county was, by himself and his deputies, to take the poll of the resident householders of his county in each parish on the same day. It appears from Flood's speech on that occasion that he also contemplated, as most of the old Reformers did contemplate, the

shortening of the duration of Parliament.
Probably with the view of diminishing opposition,
he refrained from actually proposing any disfranchisement of the existing boroughs, but he
suggested that, if any opposition were offered to
his scheme on the ground of the enlargement of
the Parliamentary body, this difficulty could be
met by taking one member from a hundred of
the smaller boroughs.

Thus we have the interesting fact that Mr.
Gladstone's measure of 1884 was anticipated by
Flood's Reform Bill brought before the House
of Commons ninety-four years ago. If some
plagiarist were to commit Flood's speech to
memory and recite it in the House of Commons
as an argument in favour of the Representation
of the People Bill, there is so little that is archaic
in the speech, and so much directly relevant to
Mr. Gladstone's proposals, that, were it not for
the knowledge that some members of Parliament at least must be assumed to possess of
the ancient debates in their House, he might,
with very little trouble, guard himself against

detection. In the following passages the alterations he would have to make would be few
indeed :—

" The members should be elected by a
numerous and a new body of responsible electors,
namely, the resident householders in every
county—resident, I say, because the representation of the constitution is so strongly in favour
of residence that it ordained that no non-
resident could be an elector, and with reason ;
first, because residents must be best acquainted
with every local circumstance ; and next because
they can attend at every place of election with
the least inconvenience and expense to themselves or candidate. Householders, I say, because being masters or fathers of families they
must be sufficiently responsible to be entitled
to franchise. There is no country in the world
in which the householders of it are considered
as the rabble—no country can be said to be
free where they are not allowed to be efficient
citizens. They are exclusive of the rabble, the
great mass of the people. They are the natural
guards of popular liberty in the first stages of
it. Without them it cannot be retained ; as

long as they have this constitutional influence, and till they become generally corrupt, popular liberty cannot be taken away. Whenever they do become generally corrupt, it cannot be retained. Neither will it be long possessed if they have not this constitutional influence, for the liberty of a nation, like the honour of individuals, can never be safe but in their own custody. The householders of this country have a better right to consideration and franchise than those of any other country, because they pay more for it. It is admitted that every individual of this country, one with another, pays fifty shillings a year to the revenue in tax. The master or father of a family must contribute in proportion for himself and for each individual of his family, even to the child that is hanging to the breast. Who shall say that this class of men ought to be confounded with the rabble? Who shall dare to say that they ought to be proscribed from franchise? They maintain the affluence of the rich, the dignity of the noble, the majesty of the crown; they support your fleets and your armies. And who shall say that they have not this right to protect their liberty. * * * Every individual pays fifty shillings a year ; how many enjoyments must every inferior individual relinquish and how much labour must he undergo to enable him to make this contribution. No people ever deserved better of Government than the people of this country at this moment ; they have not only submitted with alacrity to this enormous mass of taxation, but when the health or the rights of their sovereign were at stake they gathered around the throne with unexampled zeal. Can such a people be denied their privileges ? Can their privileges be a subject of indifference or remissness to this House ? I cannot believe it, and therefore I move ' That leave be given to bring in a Bill to amend the representation of the people in Parliament.' "

The opposition to Flood's Bill was strengthened by apprehensions which had already begun to prevail among the aristocracy with regard to the popular movement in France. Wyndham especially objected to repairing a house in a hurricane. Fox, however, who declared the measure to be the best he had yet heard suggested, retorted that no season was

more suited for repair of a house, than when a
hurricane was near and might possibly burst
forth. Burke was an opponent of the Bill, and
Pitt, though still professing a desire for reform,
irritated the reformers by siding both with those
who thought this scheme inopportune, and with
those who deemed it in itself objectionable. So
the Bill met with no success and was not even
pushed to a division.

CHAPTER V.

REFORM SOCIETIES. PERSECUTION OF REFORMERS.

WE have now reached a most stirring epoch in the history of Reform, when new societies were formed with the view of obtaining redress from Parliament and when the failure of the Legislature to satisfy the reasonable demands of the people led to a struggle of the most serious description.

In the few years succeeding Mr. Flood's motion, numerous popular societies sprang into existence, the aim of which was always Parliamentary Reform. The revolutionary proceedings in France heightened the prevailing excitement, and seems to have divided the nation into three parties. There were the two extreme parties— one driven by events on the continent into an attitude of absolute discouragement of any popular movement in this country, the other led by their own sense of injustice into the strongest sympathy with the rising of the French people, and inspired by the popular successes in France to fresh and almost frantic exertions for reform at home. A middle party saw in the gravity of passing events on the Continent, fresh reason for urging on our Parliament wise and moderate legislation.

The state of feeling is indicated by the correspondence which took place between the Society of Friends of the People, associated for the purpose of obtaining a Parliamentary Reform, and the Society of Constitutional Information. The first named society issued in April, 1792, a declaration in these terms :—

"A number of persons having seriously reviewed and considered the actual situation of public affairs and state of the kingdom, and having communicated to each their opinions on these subjects, have agreed and determined to institute a society for the purpose of proposing to Parliament and to the country, and of pro-

moting to the utmost of their power the following constitutional objects, making the preservation of the constitution on its true principles the
foundation of all their proceedings :—first, to
restore the freedom of election and a more equal
representation of the people in Parliament.
Secondly, to secure to the people a more frequent
exercise of their right of electing their representatives.   The persons who have signed their
names to this agreement think that these two
fundamental measures will furnish the power
and the means of correcting the abuses which
appear to them to have arisen from a neglect of
the acknowledged principles of the constitution,
and of accomplishing those subordinate objects
of reform which they deem to be essential to the
liberties of the people and to the good government of the kingdom."

This document was signed by Charles Grey,
M.P., and 148 others, of whom twenty-two were
members of the House of Commons. The
society met at the Freemasons' Tavern on the
first Saturday of every month during the sitting
of Parliament, and a committee to which all the

members belonged in rotation, conducted correspondence with similar societies and friends of
Parliamentary Reform generally in all parts of
the Kingdom. In an address to the people of
Great Britain, any parallel between the cases of
England and France was disputed and all idea
of resorting to similar remedies disclaimed.
The Lord John Russell of that day associated
himself with this movement; but by this time
reformers had become extremely distrustful of
the aid of members of parliament, and one day
when Lord John Russell was in the chair and
Mr. Byng, M.P., in the vice-chair, there came
before this society a letter signed by John
Cartwright, as chairman of the Society for
Constitutional Information, containing, after
congratulations on the establishment of this
Reform movement, the following significant
passage :—

" That the House of Commons itself, which is
the very subject to be reformed, should have
furnished a part of the strength of this new
institution, may ultimately afford important

advantages to the public. But it must not be disguised that at first this circumstance will necessarily be accompanied with doubts, with suspicions, with apprehensions. It is not, sir, the first time that members of that House have professed themselves Reformers. It is not the first time that they have entered into popular associations, but should they on this occasion prove faithfully instrumental in effecting a substantial reform in the representation of the people and the duration of Parliaments it will be the first time that the nation hath not found itself in error when it placed confidence in associated members of Parliament for the recovery of the constitutional and inestimable rights of the people."

The letter proceeded, evidently with the view of delicately pointing out the new society's want of any specific plan, to commend the precise declarations of the society to which the writer belonged. That society, he said, had not assumed the office of Reformer without knowing with precision what wanted reform. Then he added :—

"It left to such Reformers as Mr. Burke to talk of the people's liberties, and at the same time to deny or explain away their rights. This society sir, trusts that the purity of principle which actuated individual members of Parliament, who joined the associations that have been spoken of, will in no degree be affected by the observations which have been made upon the efficiency of these associations, but convinced that a strong impression still remains upon the minds of the people, that in general, persons who have long been accustomed to hold seats in the House of Commons under the present abuses in the representation, and whose connections are all aristocratic, must be almost more than men at once and completely to sacrifice both prejudice and unwarranted power at the altar of freedom—this society, convinced, I say, sir, of the existence of this impression, would not suffer its delicacy to stand in the way of its duty on this important occasion, but determined, with the frankness belonging to sincere affection, to warn its new brethren against a danger to which they might otherwise become exposed through mere inadvertency. That the distinguished persons who have adorned the Senate, and

F

now adorn your society, may be found equal
to the sublime effort of virtue which their situation now demands, and may on that account
receive the blessings of their country and of
mankind to the latest posterity, is the sincere,
the ardent wish of the Society for Constitutional
Information, in whose name I have the honour
to subscribe myself with great regard, sir, your
most obedient, humble servant, John Cartwright,
chairman."

To this letter, at a subsequent meeting of the
Friends of the People, the following sharp reply
was sent :—

" Sir,—Fully sensible that the Society for Constitutional Information have made no sacrifice to
delicacy in their address to us, we on our part shall
affect no disguise. Voluntary associations, not
being armed with public authority, have no
force but that of truth, no hope of success but in
the strength of reason and the concurrence of
the people.
' " We profess not to entertain a wish ' that the
great plans of public benefit, which Mr. Paine
has so powerfully recommended, will speedily

be carried into effect,' nor to amuse our fellow
citizens with the magnificent promise of obtaining for them 'the rights of the people in their
full extent :' the indefinite language of delusion,
which, by opening unbounded prospects of
political adventure, tends to destroy that public
opinion which is the support of all free governments and to excite a spirit of innovation, of
which no wisdom can foresee the effect, and no
skill direct the course. We view man as he is,
the creature of habit as well as of reason. We
think it, therefore, our bounden duty to propose
no extreme changes, which, however specious in
theory, can never be accomplished without
violence to the settled opinions of mankind, nor
attempted without endangering some of the
most estimable advantages which we confessedly
enjoy. We are convinced that the people bear
a fixed attachment to the happy form of our
government, and the genuine principles of our
constitution. These we cherish as objects of
just affection, not from any implicit reverence or
habitual superstition, but as institutions best
calculated to produce the happiness of man in
civil society ; and it is because we are convinced
that abuses are undermining and corrupting

them that we have associated for the preservation of those principles. We wish to
reform the constitution because we wish to
preserve it.

"Associations formed in the face of power, in
opposition to the interests of our present legislators, convince us that *individual security and
personal* independence are already established by
our laws. The immense accumulation of debt,
the enormous taxation of seventeen millions of
annual revenue, demonstrate that the *collective*
interests of the commuity have been neglected or
betrayed. We believe the defective constitution
of the assembly entrusted with the public purse
to be the real source of this evil. With this
view we have pledged ourselves to attempt a
timely and conciliatory reform, adhering in every
measure we may take to the fundamental principles of the constitution. According to these
acknowledged principles the people have a perfect right to possess an organ · by which the
public mind may speak in legislation, and to
bind their representatives to the interests of the
whole community by a frequent renovation of the
trust. These objects accomplished, we believe
abuses will find no protection in a genuine

representation of the people, that regulations best adapted to the public happiness will be gradually infused into our laws through the known channels of legislation, and that the agitated minds of men, resuming their confidence in parliament, will subside into a calm expectation of redress without forgetting the principles, or violating the forms of the constitution.

" These, as we think, are the views of the men detesting anarchy, yet sincere friends of the people. Your letter appears to us to be written with the view of creating distrust of our designs, to insinuate doubts of our sincerity, and to excite an early suspicion of our principles in the minds of the people. We have not, however, refused in answer to disclaim what we condemn, and to avow our real objects from the pursuit of which we will not suffer ourselves to be diverted by any controversy. We must take leave at the same time to decline all future intercourse with a Society whose views and objects, as far as we can collect them from the various resolutions and proceedings which have been published, we cannot help regarding as irreconcilable with those real interests in which you profess to inform and enlighten the people.   Signed, in the name of, and by order of the society, John Russell, chairman, Freemasons' Tavern, May 12th, 1792."

The event proved that Major Cartwright and his friends were not so far in the wrong in their distrust of members of Parliament.   Barely a month had elapsed before Lord John Russell with four others—Baker, Curwen, Dudley North and Courtenay—took umbrage at some action of the society, and made an excuse for retiring from its counsels.

Among the members of Parliament who remained faithful to the Friends of the People and advocated their cause through good and ill report, was Mr. Grey, to whose participation in these early movements a special interest must attach in the eyes of those who have cause to venerate his memory as that of the great statesman who ultimately, as Lord Grey, carried through Parliament the Great Reform Bill of 1832.

The long postponement of that great measure was primarily due to the measures now taken by Pitt's government in spite of the remonstrances of Grey, Fox, Sheridan, Erskine, and other defenders of popular rights. The alarm was first given to the Reformers by a royal proclamation for preventing tumultuous meetings and seditious writings. This proclamation was strenuously defended on the ground that the numerous political societies now in existence, were circulating alarming doctrines, and that some of them were actually in correspondence with the Jacobins. In these alleged seditious documents there is little which to the nineteenth century reader appears so very alarming. But the vagueness of the proclamation left it entirely uncertain whether the Society of Friends of the People and kindred institutions would not be ranked on the same level as the Revolution Society and other active and ostentatious partisans of the French revolutionary movement. Paine's "Rights of Man" and those letters of political societies which recommended the perusal of this work, were supposed to be principally aimed at. But the words of the proclamation described the seditious writings as those which endeavoured to raise groundless jealousies and discontents respecting the laws and "happy constitution of government, civil and religious, established in this kingdom." The Reformers therefore felt themselves justified in regarding the proclamation as a measure unfairly aiming a blow at the associations established for procuring a Parliamentary Reform. The ministry were asked why they did not meet the alleged seditious libels by prosecutions under the law, and Mr. Grey, in the frenzy of his indignation, delivered an attack on the Prime Minister which must ever be memorable for the bitterness of its invective. The political life of Pitt, he said, was a tissue of constant inconsistency. He never proposed a measure without intending to delude his hearers. He promised everything, performed nothing, studied all the arts of captivating popularity without ever intending to deserve it, and had proved himself from the first step of his political life a complete public apostate. Pitt took his punishment quietly, well content, no doubt, to regard it as a testimony that he had entirely succeeded in dividing the opposition, and indeed Grey's protests, though backed by the eloquence of Fox, could not even be carried to a division.

The check of the royal proclamation was only temporary, and, by the close of the year (1792), the country was in a great ferment. Political clubs abounded, and petitions flowed into Parliament for Reform. The excesses of the French Revolution, however, created a reaction against Reformers. Burke threw the ever-famous dagger on the floor of the House of Commons, and, exclaiming that such weapons were the means by which France would propagate freedom and fraternity, prayed that Heaven might avert her principles from English minds and her daggers from English hearts. The Reformers in vain appealed for an extension of the franchise in times so exciting. But the appeal was not, for a time, given up. In 1793 Grey called attention to an important petition from the Society of Friends, and moved for a committee to take its subject— Reform of Parliament—into consideration. We are indebted to this petition of the Friends of the People for a full exposition of the anomalies of Parliamentary representation at that date. The most striking facts may be thus grouped :—

70 members returned by 35 burgage tenures (nomination boroughs).

90 members returned by 46 places with not more than 50 voters.

37 members returned by 19 places with not more than 100 voters.

52 members returned by 26 places with not more than 200 voters.

20 members returned by Scotch counties with not more than 100 voters.

10 members returned by Scotch counties with not more than 250 voters.

15 members returned by 15 Scotch burghs with not more than 125 voters.

The above formed a majority of the House, and could thus decide all questions in the name of the people. It was complained that dissenters were necessarily deprived of the vote in about thirty boroughs where the right of voting was confined to members of the corporation. In most Scotch burghs the election of members was monopolised by the corporations, who were not even elected by the inhabitants. In the Scotch counties votes were made by parcelling out estates into lots of £400 per annum, and securing for these lots new charters in return for the original Crown charter for the estate. The holders of these charters reconveyed every right to the original granter, and only entered into the transaction for the purpose of obtaining the vote which belonged to what was called the superiority. 150 members of the House owed their elections entirely to peers. Complaint was made generally that property, whether well or ill employed, had equal power; and of the necessity for some further popular control upon the legislature proof was given in the shape of appalling facts as to the rapid growth of the public expenditure and corruption. These facts are here for convenience put in tabular form :—

	PUBLIC REVENUE.	PEACE ESTA-BLISHMENT.	Number of Statutes found necessary to preserve the freedom of Parliament, to regulate elections, and to prevent frauds, bribery,&c.
	£	£	
At the Revolution	2,100,000	1,900,000	14
At Wm. III.'s death	3,950,000	1,950,0:0	26
At Queen Anne's death	6,000,000	2,000,000	35
At George I.'s death	6,800,000	2,600,000	37
At George II.'s death	8,600,000	2,800,000	49
In 31st year of Geo. III.	16,000,000	5,000,000	65

Grey's motion was urged upon the House in vain. Though supported by men whose names shine out with brilliancy in the records of our Parliamentary history, he was defeated by a great majority.

Ere this, however, a spirit had arisen among the populace that was not to be quelled by Parliamentary defeat, and ministers having declined to give way to moderate demands, had to face popular passion with the severest measures of repression. Fortunately for them—unfortunately for the cause of Reform—the fears excited by the French excesses strengthened the hands of the ministry, and shielded them from censure for conduct which cannot now be regarded as otherwise than cruel in the extreme. In Scotland crushing sentences of banishment were passed on men (Muir and Palmer) whose spirited exertions in the cause of Reform were declared to be sedition, and the severity of whose punishment was in vain challenged in the Parliament of so powerful a minister as Pitt, even though it was pointed out that their crimes were but the repetition of sentiments with which Pitt and Richmond had themselves been associated a dozen years or so before. A similar punishment overtook Skirving, Margarot and Gerald, who had carried their enthusiasm to the extent of actively participating in the promotion of a great popular Convention at Edinburgh, which upon very indirect and indeed altogether inferential evidence was deemed to be a seditious assembly. The names of these martyrs of Reform are hardly recognised now-a-days. In the pages of history they have not as yet had a sufficiently prominent part. But now that the principles they avowed, with only that warmth and impetuosity which the exciting circumstances of the day and their deep sense of injustice should be sufficient to excuse—now that these principles are held almost in their full extent by at least one minister of the Crown, now that the people have at length almost won those rights for which these men struggled, their names and their sufferings ought not to be forgotten. When the tale of their misfortunes shall some day be fully told, their memories may be perpetuated with such pride and reverence as shall make fitting reparation for a previous wrong. The Convention which these Scottish martyrs promoted, had become a favourite project with all the Reformers who had wearied of vain petitioning to the House of Commons. The warning of Pitt, in his own Reform days, declaring that nothing

was to be expected from Parliament, but that
the people themselves must force the question
forward, was now remembered against him.
But the idea of a Convention was greatly fostered
by one of Paine's publications, which the government, in spite of numerous prosecutions, had the
greatest difficulty in suppressing. This was his
"Letter to the addressers of the late proclamation." A reference to this publication does not
at all prove the theory of the state prosecutions
of those days that this Convention was proposed
as a substitute for Parliament. It was merely to
be an instrument to ascertain the sense of the
nation and to convey it with no uncertain
sound to Parliament. The argument was that
neither elections in the manner in which they
were then conducted, nor addresses from rotten
boroughs, nor county meetings promoted by
placemen and pensioners could convey to the
Parliament the sense of the people. By a
national Convention Paine intended that the
general will, whether to reform or not, what "the
reform should be or how far it should extend,

should be known." It could not, he said, be known by any other means. The London Corresponding Society and its numerous divisions in the country favoured this project. That it was partially carried out was of course due to the failure of government to meet the popular demand in any way. That the Convention was characterised by extravagances, and that it should have copied the forms of the French Convention need not be surprising, considering the excitement of the times, but that it had any aims beyond that of obtaining a Parliamentary Reform and of taking steps to resist attacks upon popular liberty was never proved. It was only after this Convention was forcibly suppressed that any whisper was heard of schemes of violence; and the treasonable scheme for the seizure of Edinburgh castle, for which a man named Watt was tried and executed, was never brought home to the political societies who were said to be privy to it. In England the government failed to obtain convictions against Horne Tooke, Hardy, and Thelwall, leaders in the Crusade of the

Reformers. The Ministry, in their contest with the popular fervour, had procured against the strongest protests, the repeal of the Habeas Corpus Act. Notwithstanding the powerful weapon thus placed in the hands of the executive, public meetings increased, and new societies were formed to procure " Peace, Reform, and Cheap Bread." A monster meeting of these Reformers in Copenhagen Fields was somehow or other connected with an outrage on the king at the opening of Parliament, and the Government obtained in consequence fresh powers for dealing with so-called seditious meetings and treasonable practices. These for the moment practically put an end to the struggle for Reform. Fox, Grey and Sheridan declared that if these bills were passed, the propriety of resistance, instead of remaining any longer a question of morality, would become merely a question of prudence. But prudence seems to have dictated a sullen acquiescence in the inevitable, and the only gratification left to the Reformers was their hearty execration of Pitt and his ministers. For

years the country was governed only with the
aid of coercive measures.   When Lord Holland
was reproached for reviling the Constitution, he
repudiated the charge, on the ground that he
would never speak ill of the dead !

CHAPTER VI.

LEADING UP TO 1831.

IN the preceding Chapters there have been presented to the reader past schemes of Reform, embracing not only all the principles of modern legislation, but nearly all the proposals which have been speculatively advanced by modern writers and speakers on the subject of representation. Minority Representation has not, of course, come to the front. Our forefathers suffered too much and too long from the representation of nothing but a minority, to think much about that in their plans of reform. Payment of members too is still in the background. The old Reformers, looking back as they did to the ancient Constitution, must all have known that payment of members was formerly the rule of the Constitution, but up to the time we have now reached few had the boldness to propose a reversion to that system in times when the chief complaint against the existing House of Commons was the expense in which its policy involved the people. But there actually had been a curious scheme published by Horne Tooke, in which both payment of members and favourable treatment of the wealthy minority by a system of plurality of votes were provided for. The proposal indeed embodied many other curious ideas. It was mooted in a letter to Lord Ashburton just after Pitt's celebrated motion when men were comparing his plan of moderate reform as it was called, with the radical reform insisted upon by Major Cartwright and others. Tooke accepted Cartwright's principle, that every man had an equal right to a share in representation, but he disputed every man's right to an equal share.

Starting from this position, Tooke's plan seems to have combined the principles of equal electoral districts, manhood rating suffrage, annual elections, plurality of votes, payment of members, and

payment for the privilege of voting. Of course the
stipulation of a payment by the voter must have
been at the very outset an insuperable obstacle to
the consideration of the scheme by those ardent
Reformers who claimed the vote for every man,
rich or poor, as a right. Tooke suggested the division of the country into as many districts as there
were members. The number was then 513. Every
male native of the age of 21, who had been rated
for the space of the preceding year to the land-
tax or parish rates at £2 per annum, was to be
entitled to vote in his own district on his paying
to the presiding officer the sum of two guineas.
Four thousand votes, yielding at this rate £8,400,
had nominally to be polled in every constituency.
If the four thousand votes were not polled in the
first instance a second chance of voting at the
same price was given to all that portion of the
constituency which was rated at £20. If the
votes still fell short of the required number,
persons rated at £50 and upwards had the
privilege of voting a third time on payment of
their two guineas, and so on till a class was

reached who might actually vote six times. Thus the wealthy minority could in any con- stituency take advantage of the lack of public spirit on the part of the voters below them in social position, and secure the return of their own man.   When all this complicated voting was at an end, and the sheriff still found that he had not got 4,000 votes and the accompanying £8,400, the balance was to be made up by a rate levied on all people rated at £20 and upwards who had ne- glected to vote.   The member was to be allowed to take his seat when he could produce a receipt from the Exchequer for £8,000.   The odd £400 was to be given to him as his annual payment. Tooke's idea was that the £8,000 paid into the Exchequer for every elected member would be available in cases of national emergency such as war, and so relieve the burdens of the people. We have thus before the end of last century the whole ground of Reform thoroughly broken, so that the remainder of the story prior to 1831 need not take up long time.   But before re- suming the narrative of action in the Legislature it may be interesting first here to follow up the account of Horne Tooke's eccentric plan of Reform by some description of another scheme elaborated by Jeremy Bentham, which was published early in the present century. He revived the demand for a Radical Reform, and gave prominence to the important proposal of vote by ballot. He frankly owned democratic ascendency as the object he had in view. He pointed out that the democratic interest really meant the universal interest, and that when this was subordinated to the monarchical and aristocratic interest the result would be a tendency to a monarchy virtually absolute. He ridiculed the notion of a balance of power in the Constitution. When forces balanced each other, he said, the machine came to a stand. He traced what he called the mischief of misrule to the fact that members of Parliament were at one and the same time unduly independent of the people, and unduly dependent on the Ministers. To provide against the evil, he proposed that they should be annually elected by universal suffrage, or virtually universal suffrage, the votes being secret, and taken on the same day. Bentham thought he was the first to introduce the question of the ballot. He forgot Major Cartwright's advocacy of this scheme; but he seems to have been the the first to open the question of Woman Suffrage. This hitherto has not been included in the term Universal Suffrage. Fox declared in one of his speeches, that it had never been in the contemplation of the most absurd theorists to extend the elective franchise to the female sex. Bentham, when he first stated his plan, did not express a decided opinion in regard to this question, but he discussed it in such a manner as to have elevated it from that time onwards into the rank of at least debateable questions. A curious feature in Bentham's plan was a proposition that the members of Parliament should be required to be in constant attendance. This proposal, if one could conceive it possible to put it in force at the present day, might at least have the merit of giving members a strong interest in curtailing each other's speeches within reasonable limits.

Returning now to the House of Commons, it is noteworthy that in 1797 the subject of household suffrage was once again introduced, this time on the motion of Mr. Grey. According to his plan, no fewer than 400 members were to be elected by the householders of the kingdom. He proposed to divide the country into districts, to adopt what we in the present day would call the one-man-one-vote principle, and to limit the duration of Parliament to three years. There were to be 113 county members, and the right of election, which was then confined to freeholders, was to be extended to copyholders and leaseholders for a certain number of years. He laid down the principle that "great towns such as the metropolis, should require a greater number of electors to return a representative than places where the population was more scattered, otherwise the populous towns would obtain a too great local ascendency." This scheme received very high praise from Fox, who

it will be remembered had also given his approbation to Flood's scheme. He said, " I think
that to extend the right of election to housekeepers is the best and most advisable plan of
reform.   I think also that it is the most perfect
recurrence to first principles.   I do not mean to
the first principles of society, nor the abstract
principles of representation, but to the first
known and recorded principles of our Constitution.   According to the early history of England and the highest authorities on our parliamentary constitution, I find this to be the case.
It is the opinion of the celebrated Glanville
that in all cases where no particular right
intervenes, the common law right of paying scot
and lot, was the right of election in the land
. . . . . and this in my opinion is the safest line
of conduct you can adopt."   Mr. Grey obtained
ninety-three votes in favour of his motion,
but it was opposed by 258 and was consequently lost.

On the union with Ireland, Grey took objection to the introduction of one hundred Irish

representatives, but not on the ground upon which some members are to-day disposed to object to the proportion of Irish members. He did not fear the popular party. He apprehended, from the nature of Irish elections, that the influence of the Crown in the Parliament would be unduly increased. But being unwilling to alter the proposed ratio between British and Irish representatives, he suggested that forty of our most decayed boroughs should be disfranchised, so as to cut off eighty-eight English members. The proportion to which Ireland would then be entitled would be eighty-five, of whom sixty-nine would come from the Irish counties, and the remaining sixteen be chosen by popular election in the principal towns. This proposal also was defeated, and we hear little more of Grey in the capacity of Reformer until the great measure of 1831.

In the meantime the sale of seats was becoming a greater scandal than ever, and by 1809 this state of affairs had revived the outdoor agitation for Reform. It was in this year that Sir Francis Burdett first brought forward his scheme of Reform, which was, that free-holders, householders, and others, subject to direct taxation in support of the poor, the Church, and the State, should be the electors; that counties should be divided into districts, each returning one representative; that all the elections should be taken in one day, and that Parliaments should be brought back to their constitutional duration.

Mr. Brand in 1810 outlined a plan by which, in the counties, copyholders were to be enfranchised, and the vote in the metropolis and other populous places was to be given to all house-holders paying parochial and other taxes. The nomination boroughs were to be disfranchised. It was pointed out by the same member in 1812, that in the House of Commons, as it then existed, 326 members were returned by 182 individuals.

The stirring events of war kept the Reform agitation for a little while in the background, but in 1817, at a time when there was much distress among the people, the cause of Reform received a great stimulus from the writings of Cobbett, whose " Weekly Register," reduced in price, was now circulated widely among the working classes. Again the political clubs became active all over the country, and again they were assailed by Government declaring that under the pretence of Parliamentary Reform, they aimed at nothing short of revolution. The Habeas Corpus Act was once more suspended, and bills for preventing seditious meetings were passed. These clubs, some of them known as Hampden, others as Spencean clubs, were entered by spies and informers, who actually incited their members to treasonable acts.

The story of this period, as found in some recent histories of the present century, and especially in the personal narratives of Bamford and Prentice, arouses at once the pity and the indignation of the reader. With compassion we picture the procession of the Blanketeers—simple men, imagining themselves with their blankets and their petitions efficiently equipped for a

march from Manchester to London, to make
known their distress to the Prince Regent, and
obtain relief from a Parliamentary Reform.
With indignation we burn at the brutal manner
of their dispersion miles from their homes,
at their wounds, and at their imprisonment.
That despair should have driven some of
the poverty-stricken working-men in the north
to mad projects of force only deepens the impression of their misery, for it is not to be
forgotten that, at this time, the evils of misgovernment had continued for a quarter of a
century after the time when Fox and Grey were
declaring that prudence alone could supply the
motive for refraining from resistance. The
marvel is that prudence so generally prevailed,
in spite of the instigation of government spies,
in spite of the distress caused by the corn laws,
in spite of the repressive measures of the Tory
Ministry. Parliament continued deaf to all constitutional appeals. Romilly and Brougham
tried for the repeal of the Septennial Act in
vain. When Burdett brought forward resolu-

tions in favour of annual Parliaments, universal suffrage, and nearly equal electoral districts, he was not even met with any offer of compromise. He and his co-teller, Lord Cochrane, had no votes to tell, while their resolutions were negatived by 124. There was not now the same excuse for refusing to deal with the demands for Reform. It could not be urged now that the agitation was that of the lowest classes, and had not the sympathy of responsible citizens. The corporation of London had, more than a year before Sir F. Burdett's resolutions, petitioned the Prince Regent to "restore the people to their just weight in the Legislature," and other petitions were sent to Parliament in great numbers. It being impossible to move Parliament by ordinary means, the Reformers in the great towns began to take a striking means of indicating their determination to have some kind of representative. A meeting of 50,000 persons at Birmingham elected Sir Charles Wolseley the "legislatorial attorney and representative" for that borough, and required him to go and claim

his seat in the House of Commons. The closing
of the Parliament on the following day, and the
arrest of Birmingham's nominee, prevented Sir
Charles's obedience to these instructions. In the
meantime, Lord Sidmouth, the Home Secretary
of that day, instructed the Lords Lieutenants of
counties to watch the Reform meetings, and to
have yeomanry in readiness to preserve the
peace. As great Reform meetings were now
being held all over the country, the responsibility
of the authorities who had to carry out these
instructions was serious. The Manchester
authorities attained an odious distinction in
their discharge of this duty.

The Manchester Reformers had desired to
appoint Mr. Henry Hunt as their legislatorial
attorney. Orator Hunt, as he was called, shared
with Cobbett and Burdett the honours of popularity as a leader of the Reform movement.
The magistrates forbade the meeting at which
Hunt was to be nominated the people's representative, and the Reformers proposed to substitute a town's meeting in favour of Reform.

The authorities declining to call this meeting, it was resolved.to hold a great open-air demonstration at St. Peter's Fields, Manchester, a site now partially covered by that scene of many hundreds of great popular meetings since—the Free Trade Hall. To the meeting came the members of many political clubs of the town and surrounding country, carrying flags and banners with such mottoes as "Annual Parliaments," " Universal Suffrage," and "Vote by Ballot." Two clubs of female Reformers joined the processions, and wives, sweethearts, and sisters accompanying the men were guarantees of peaceable intentions. The crowd, consisting of some 50,000 persons, had gathered round the waggon which formed the hustings, to hear the address of Orator Hunt, the chairman of the day, when the Yeomanry came up, flourishing their swords, and demanded that Hunt should surrender. Hunt quietly complied with the summons. A cry was then heard " Have at the flags." This came from the Yeomanry, described as hot-headed young men who had volunteered from their intense hatred of Radicalism. " Instantly " says one writer,* "the yeomen drew their swords, waved them in the air, and dashed into the dense crowd. The astonished and defenceless crowd gave way so far as it could ; but necessarily swaying to and fro the horsemen's ranks were broken, and themselves swamped in that living sea. The commander of the Hussars says that it was at this juncture he was called upon ; and that he saw at a glance the yeomen were ' in the power of those whom they were designed to overawe.' His troop were ordered to the rescue, and though careful to use the backs of their sabres, appalling were the wounds they inflicted. ' People, yeomen, and constables,' says the officer, ' in their confused attempts to escape ran one over the other, so that by the time we had arrived at the end of the field, the fugitives were literally piled up to a considerable elevation above the level of the field.' Even then the havoc was scarcely begun. The brutal yeomen,

* Washington Wilks, in "The Half Century."

infuriated at being indebted for rescue to the regular soldiery, wheeled, dashed in at every opening, and struck right and left. . . . Eight men, two women, and a child, were taken up before night, dead or mortally injured. The wounded had fled or been carried by hundreds to their homes . . . A committee was formed at Manchester, and attended by a deputation from London, to release the wounded and defend the imprisoned. Five hundred and sixty cases of serious injury were reported by the committee. And this was only an approximation to the whole truth, for of the numbers of poor creatures who had refused to apply for parish or surgical aid lest their wounds should be made witnesses against them, many kept back even from the relief committee. One hundred and forty, fourteen of whom were women, had received sabre cuts, and a hundred and thirteen other women had been severely bruised by sabre or hoof. The gentle forbearance of the cruelly outraged people, whose numerical might was after all overwhelming, and whose vengeance no amount of physical force could have suppressed, was a keen reproach on those who vilified and oppressed them even unto blood. It is infinitely to the honour of the working classes of that day, that their six hundred killed and wounded were smitten down unarmed, and were not avenged by midnight burnings nor private assassinations." This stirring episode in the history of Reform was long popularly known by the name of The Massacre of Peterloo.

The immediate result of Peterloo was only the further persistence in repressive measures. The popular leaders, including Orator Hunt, were imprisoned. The famous six acts—measures for prevention of so-called sedition—were passed. Even the moderate reform resolutions of Lord John Russell were not accepted. But Lord John had the satisfaction of soon afterwards dealing the first blow at the rotten boroughs, and thus procuring the first instalment of reform. He obtained the disfranchisement of the borough of Grampound. In this Cornish borough, the right of returning two members to Parliament, was

nominally vested in forty-two electors—the corporation and freemen. The freemen of this
borough had boasted of receiving 300 guineas a
man for their votes ; and one of the aldermen
had confessed to a committee of the House of
Commons that there were not more than three
or four uncorrupt electors in the whole place.
The demand for the disfranchisement of this
borough was too overpowering to be successfully·
resisted, but the endeavour to bestow its two
members upon Leeds, and thus to give one large
town a ·representation in Parliament, was frustrated. The members were added to those
representing the county of York.

. In the same year in which Grampound was
disfranchised, Mr Lambton (afterwards Lord
Durham) took courage once again to draw
attention to the utter effacement of the popular
representation in the House of Commons, to
emphasise the fact that 350 members of that
House were returned by 180 individuals, and to
propose to Parliament that a committee should
consider the state of representation with a view

to the passing of a Household Suffrage bill. He proposed to give the right of election to all inhabitant householders, *bonâ fide* rated, paying rates and taxes, for six months before the election, and never having received parochial relief. To the county electorate he desired to add copyholders and leaseholders. The duration of Parliament he proposed to make triennial.

For years after this Lord John Russell was the champion of reform of a comparatively moderate type, and was supported by a vast number of petitions, but the corrupt Parliament naturally enough refused persistently to decree its own reform. At length, the hands of the reformers were strengthened, ludicrously enough, by a Tory cry. The upholders of the rotten borough system were bitten by it. It had long before been pointed out, that the system of corruption was a two-edged weapon, and that, for example, the dissenters who were excluded from office, could if they chose by an organised attempt to secure sufficient influence in the rotten boroughs, obtain a majority in the House of Commons. Now, the

Tories, who were maddened by the concessions of Wellington and Peel to the demand for Catholic emancipation, began to rail against the influence the ministry possessed in the rotten boroughs. One of their number—the Marquis of Blandford—actually associated himself with O'Connell in bringing forward a motion of Reform. He contemplated the disfranchisement of the decayed boroughs, the adoption of household suffrage, and the payment of members at £2 a day for borough representatives, and £4 for knights of the shire. The motion met with the fate of all its predecessors.

Ireland, it should be particularly noted here, was the victim of a disfranchising act in the year of the Catholic Relief Bill. Upon the plea that by the creation of small freeholders a great many votes had been placed at the command of the landlords and priests, the freehold qualification was raised from forty shillings to £10.

Lord John Russell failed in 1830 to enfranchise Leeds, Birmingham, and Manchester, but he was only defeated by 188 votes to 140; and now the day of reform began to dawn. Brougham had prophetically said, "The schoolmaster is abroad, and I trust more to the schoolmaster armed with his primer than I do to the soldier in full military array, for upholding and extending the liberties of my country." The people were rapidly learning the exact measure of their servitude. Hume's persistent attacks on financial abuses aroused popular sympathy and freshened their interest in political reform. Then O'Connell lost a motion in favour of universal suffrage, triennial parliaments, and vote by ballot; but a watchword was given to the reformers of the Kingdom by the Duke of Newcastle, which became a powerful weapon of ridicule against the pretensions of the borough-mongers, and greatly forwarded the popular cause. The more independent electors of Newark had complained of his Grace's dictation. The Duke was astounded at any proposal to interfere with what he regarded as his rights, and exclaimed in the House of Lords, "May I not do what I will with mine own?" The phrase became an educative bye-word, and for many a day the popular orator drew a ready laugh with the mock inquiry—"May I not do what I will with mine own?"

A great stimulus was given to the English reform movement by the French revolution of 1830. At the general election ministers could not get seats in the more popular constituencies. Brougham was returned, pledged to Parliamentary Reform, by the freeholders of Yorkshire. Hume was returned by Middlesex. Forty-seven out of eighty-two county members were reformers, and only three out of twenty-eight city members were ministerialists.

On the first night of the new session—2nd November, 1830,—an important interchange of opinion passed between the Prime Minister—the Duke of Wellington—and the leader of the opposition—Earl Grey—which sounded the first notes of challenge in the great political conflict of the century. Lord Grey, noticing that in the distressed state of the country, the people, having no legitimate means of appeal for redress, were resorting to brick throwing and other violent measures, asked what remedies the ministry had in view. "We see," he said, "the hurricane approaching. We may trace presages of the storm on the verge of the horizon. What course ought we to adopt? We should put our house in order; we should secure our door against the tempest. How? By securing ourselves of the affection of our subjects, by removing grievances, by affording redress, by—may I venture to use the word?—the adoption of the measures of temperate reform. I know not whether we can expect the ministers will undertake such measures, but of this I am satisfied, that if they do not make up their minds to the course indicated in time, it will be ultimately forced upon them and reform will be carried under circumstances much less safe and advantageous than now present themselves. I have been a reformer all my life, and I will add that never in my younger days, when I might be supposed to have entertained projects wilder or more extensive than mature years and increased experience would sanction, never would I have pressed reform further than I would do now were the opportunity offered."

The reply of the Duke of Wellington was uncompromising. "I am fully convinced," he said, "that the country possesses at the present moment a Legislature which answers all the good purposes of legislation, and this to a greater degree than any Legislature ever has answered in any country whatever. I am not only not prepared to bring forward any measure of the description alluded to by the noble lord, but I will at once declare that so far as I am concerned, and as long as I hold my station in the government of the country, I shall always feel it my duty to resist such measures when proposed by others." The ministry was more discredited than ever by this declaration and did not long survive it. Not many days afterwards the Duke of Wellington resigned and Earl Grey took office, pledged to introduce to Parliament a scheme of Parliamentary Reform.

CHAPTER VII.

THE REFORM BILL OF 1831.

WHEN Earl Grey took office it was every day becoming more evident that no half measure of reform would satisfy the country. The lower and middle classes had begun to unite in their demands for an improved representation. Their political unions were obtaining a power and influence which could not but be significant in the eyes of ministers ; and, most alarming feature of all, the idea of withholding taxes until the popular demand received due attention, was beginning to be discussed with favour. The newspapers were vigorously advocating reform, and exposing the abuses of the representation with great effect. The enormous cost of elections was disgusting even some of those who before might have fancied themselves interested in objecting to reform. This feeling, combined with the extraordinary pressure of public opinion, secured the return of a larger number of members in favour of reform than was expected ; and, though a momentous struggle had to be undergone before the final triumph of the reformers, the old system of election was now doomed.

How much the country owed to Earl Grey for conducting it safely through the terrible crisis could not be fully realized by his contemporaries. Some of the Reformers had ceased to trust him because of what they conceived to have been his extremely doubtful and lukewarm attitude on this subject ever since 1810. As for Lord John Russell they never associated with his name any idea of a reform so extensive as that he was about to propose, and the only Reformers in the new and mixed ministry whom they were disposed to trust were Lord Durham and Lord Brougham. Even the latter they would have regarded with some uncertainty now he had taken office, had he not been so deeply committed by his pledges to the Yorkshire electors, and his public assurances to

the House of Commons in giving notice of a
Reform Bill just before the dissolution. To show
that there was some justification for the distrust
of Earl Grey, the Reformers afterwards pointed
to his own declaration in the House of Lords,
that the scheme of Reform he originally contemplated was comprised within much narrower
limits.   However that may be, Earl Grey did
make himself responsible for a far-reaching
measure, and to-day there are proofs which the
Reformers of 1831 did not possess of Lord Grey's
thorough loyalty to the cause of the people.
They are proofs of a kind which could not well
be produced in the reigning King's lifetime ; and
their production since teaches how important it
is not to assume that, in criticising the conduct of
popular ministers of the Crown, all the material
for an impartial judgment is to be found
in their public acts.   The fuller knowledge
enjoyed by the present generation of Earl Grey's
services to the people in connection with the
Reform question is due to the publication, some
years ago, of the letters which passed between

him and the King.* The "Sailor King," who was for a while so popular, and whom the people at one time called their Reform *Bill,* was a more reluctant supporter of the Reform policy of his ministry than was generally supposed, or even than he himself would have cared to admit. He yielded much. At the same time every page of his letters tells of his reluctance to move, or his misgivings for moving. On the other hand, every letter of Earl Grey's is a testimony to that stateman's tact in the trying task of arguing with his King, and a monument of his masterly ability in the advocacy of the popular cause. Lord Grey had to approach the subject in the most gingerly fashion. Writing to the King's secretary letters which it was understood would be brought under His Majesty's notice, he spoke of Parliamentary Reform as "the perilous question" of the day. "Public opinion," he wrote, "is so strongly directed to this question, and so generally, that it cannot be resisted with-

* "The Correspondence of the late Earl Grey with His Majesty King William the Fourth," &c. : John Murray.

out the greatest danger of leaving the government in a position in which it would be deprived of all authority and strength. Under this impression I must naturally feel the greatest anxiety on a subject which it is plain that His Majesty contemplates with so much apprehension and uneasiness." The fact was, the Cabinet * had remitted the consideration of this great question to a Committee, consisting of Lord Durham, Sir J. R. Graham, Lord John Russell, and Lord Duncannon—all holding offices under Lord Grey; and the measure which they had recommended as necessary to satisfy the reason-

* The Cabinet was thus made up :—Earl Grey, First Lord of the Treasury; Lord Brougham, Lord Chancellor ; Viscount Althorp, Chancellor of the Exchequer ; Marquis of Lansdowne, President of the Council ; Lord Durham, Lord Privy Seal ; Viscount Melbourne, Home Secretary ; Viscount Palmerston, Foreign Secretary ; Viscount Goderich, Colonial Secretary ; Sir J. R. Graham, First Lord of the Admiralty ; Lord Auckland, Master of the Mint ; Mr. C. Grant, President of the Board of Trade ; Duke of Richmond, Postmaster-General ; Lord Holland, Chancellor of the Duchy of Lancaster ; and the Earl of Carlisle.

able demands of the public was a more extensive scheme than probably the King had ever
dreamt of. The nomination boroughs were
ruthlessly condemned. The Committee could
consider no measure otherwise than trifling or
nugatory which did not include their abolition
or purification. They proposed to disfranchise
all boroughs with a population under 2000 ; to
deprive of one member every borough having
a population under 4000 ; to lessen the chances
of corruption by the extension of the franchise
in boroughs where it was at the time enjoyed by
the corporation, or by a limited number of voters ;
to give representatives to all large and populous
towns of more than ten thousand inhabitants ;
to give additional members to the more populous counties ; to extend the right of voting in
counties to leaseholders of £50 holdings and
copyholders at £10 per annum ; to enforce
residence ; to register all voters ; to adopt the
ballot, to increase the number of polling sta-
tions, to shorten the period of election, and to
limit the duration of Parliament to five years.

The King was greatly averse both to the ballot
and the curtailment of the period for which members of Parliament were elected.   He afterwards
avowed that he would never have consented to
the bill had the Cabinet included a provision for
the ballot in it.   The Cabinet omitted any such
provision ; but they included in the proposals
first submitted to the King a clause shortening
the duration of Parliaments in accordance with
their Committee's recommendation.   The King,
while professing to waive his objections to this
proposal, strongly hinted his desire for its withdrawal, and in the end it found no place in the
Ministerial Bill.   While these measures were in
this manner opposed by the King, it was
obvious that he dreaded even those to which he
assented.   He feared an increased popularity of
the Lower House by "the substitution of a
representation of numbers for one of property."
It was his wish that the forty-shilling freeholder
qualification should be altered into a £10 qualification ; and he showed a strong anxiety lest
the Cabinet should fix the town qualification too

low to be consistent with his views regarding the
maintenance of an equilibrium between the
representation of property and numbers. Earl
Grey skilfully soothed the feelings of the King,
and His Majesty, pleased for the moment that
greater concessions to a growing clamour in the
country had been averted, promised Lord Grey at
the outset his utmost support in what he acknowledged to be a period of unexampled difficulty.
But ever and anon his anxieties revealed themselves afresh, and Lord Grey had to deal most
diplomatically with his tendencies towards
repentance for concessions made.

The Reform Bill was introduced by Lord
John Russell on the 1st March, 1831. Lord
John was not a Cabinet Minister—his office was
that of Paymaster of the Forces—but Lord
Althorp, the leader of the House of Commons,
had ceded the honour to him in accordance with
an announcement, which he had gracefully made
to the House a month previously, that Lord
John had been selected, in consequence of
the deep sense the Government entertained of

the ability and perseverance with which he had
advocated the improvement of the representative
system through the whole course of his public life.
So Lord John had the honour of expounding
the provisions of a measure of unexampled
public importance to a specially crowded and
anxious House, and to galleries, the places in
which had been so eagerly fought for, that the
Speaker had only obtained order on a threat to
clear the Chamber of strangers. The principle
on which he rested in explaining the measure,
was that the House of Commons should
represent the people of England. He asked his
hearers to imagine the surprise of the stranger,
who, hearing of our representative institutions,
should come to see the places of election and
find that a green mound returned two members to Parliament, that a similar right of
election attached to a stone wall with three
niches in it, and that from another place with a
green park and no habitation, two members
were sent to the House of Commons. He
pictured the increased surprise of the stranger,

when he was taken to the flourishing and populous manufacturing towns of the country, and informed that they had no representatives. He maintained that it would be easier to transfer the manufactures of Leeds and Manchester to Gatton and Old Sarum, than to re-establish confidence and sympathy between the existing House of Commons and the country. Three grievances he urged must be redressed. The nomination of members by individuals must be stopped. Elections by close corporations must cease. The expense of election must be diminished. These being the evils to be met, his cure was drastic. First it was proposed that 60 boroughs, returning two members each, should be disfranchised. These were all small boroughs with a population for the most part far below 2000, and in which elections were either completely under the control of the proprietor of the borough, or were regularly manipulated by bribery. Forty-seven more boroughs with fewer than 4000 inhabitants were to be dispossessed of one of their two members.

Weymouth, which had sent four members since its union with Melcombe Regis in the reign of Queen Elizabeth, although it had only some seven or eight hundred voters, was condemned to give up two of its representatives. These were all the nominal proposals of disfranchisement, but the provisions of the bill, which dealt with the qualifications of electors, necessarily implied disfranchisement of many electors in those towns where the election was open. The fact was, that the intention of the Ministry to extend the franchise to several large towns which up to this time had no member, would have necessitated that excessive representation of numbers of which the King, and no doubt a number of ministers, were equally afraid, unless some franchise was fixed which should be different from that now existing in the open boroughs. Hitherto the franchise, in whatever way limited, had not in any borough been associated with any fixed payment. The burgage holder in the towns was the equivalent of the freeholder in the counties. When householders as such were entitled. to vote, the only qualification was that implied in the term "scot and lot householders," or inhabitants contributing to the parish rates. In some places all the inhabitants had the right of voting. In others, what was practically the same thing, the right belonged to those who were called " potwallopers," or " pot-wallers," or " pot-boilers "—that is, all who made the pot boil, whether lodgers or householders, all in fact who maintained themselves without relief from the parish rates.* The Ministry felt bound to

---

* The qualifications for voting prior to 1832, were so various in the different boroughs as almost to defy classification. Some idea of the variety of voting rights may be gained from the following list, in which each item is a description of the voters in a different town :—

Freemen burgesses and resident and non-resident householders not receiving alms.

Scot and lot householders not receiving alms.

Scot and lot householders.

Mayor, aldermen, bailiffs, and eighteen burgesses and inhabitants paying scot and lot, not receiving alms.

Householders not receiving alms.

Corporation.

Mayor, bailiffs and burgesses not receiving alms.

Mayor, bailiffs, and freemen.

demolish the worst boroughs, and to open up
others, in which the right of election was confined
to corporations, or to a very few citizens who had
proved themselves open to corruption, but they
were not prepared to allow a franchise so liberal
as they found in these potwalloping constituencies.   Indeed, if they had been so inclined,

Resident freemen.

Mayor and burgesses resident or non-resident.

Freeholders and leaseholders for 99 years resident
40 days within the borough and paying rates, also householders, after a residence of six months.

Burgage tenants.

Corporation, freemen and sworn burgesses.

Inhabitant householders.

Rated inhabitants and non-residents rated on real
estates.

Citizens and freemen resident.

Freemen and inhabitants.

Inhabitants at large (Preston).

The livery (London city).

Scot and lot payers (as Westminster and Southwark).

Freemen and householders (Bristol).

Potwallers not receiving alms (Taunton).

Freemen by birth, servitude or redemption.

Persons paying to church or poor.

Freemen by servitude not receiving alms.

they would probably have found the task altogether beyond their strength. The fact was that in the potwalloping constituencies there was too much of that bribery and corruption to which it was the professed object of the bill to put an end; and though present-day Radicals may urge that it was the limited size of these free constituencies that made them so open to bribery, and point to the fact that in such large constituencies as Preston and Westminster, the voters had returned members upon purer principles, we can easily understand how greatly the difficulties of ministers would have been increased in those days, if they had attempted to confer the franchise upon the multitude in the towns. In the ministerial bill, therefore, it was proposed that all existing rights of voting should die out with the voters of that day, and cease at once to be exercised, if the voters did not reside in the borough; and that a new set of voters should be immediately created, viz., those paying rates for or occupying a house of the yearly value of £10. A less liberal franchise would have been proposed (so Lord John candidly confessed) had it not been discovered that by fixing the limit at £20, as was originally contemplated, the franchise would be so much restricted in some of the smaller boroughs, as practically to create afresh a number of those close boroughs which it was the primary object of the bill to destroy. So here we have the first appearance on the Reform platform of the £10 householder.

At this time, with the exception of the City, Southwark, and Westminster, the populous metropolitan districts were without any representation except such as was enjoyed by those qualified to vote for the counties. It was now proposed to create four new metropolitan boroughs with two members each :—

Tower Hamlets.	Finsbury.
Holborn.	Lambeth.

Up to this time also, the following large towns had been unrepresented, though their population in 1821 was as here stated :—

Manchester and Salford . . .	133,788
Birmingham and Aston	104,605
Leeds	86,746
Greenwich, Deptford, and Woolwich .	56,582
Wolverhampton, Bilston, and Sedgeley	66,036
Sheffield	62,105
Sunderland and the Wearmouths . .	33,911

To each of these seven great urban communities, the bill proposed to give two members.
To the following towns, whose population ranged
from ten to thirty thousand and was rapidly
increasing, the bill proposed to give one
member :—

Brighton.

Blackburn.

Macclesfield.

South Shields and Westoe.

Warrington.

Huddersfield.

Halifax.

Gateshead.

Whitehaven, Working-
ton, and Harrington.

Kendal.

Bolton.

Stockport.

Dudley.

Tynemouth and North
Shields.

Cheltenham. .

Bradford.

Frome.

Wakefield.

Kidderminster.

Walsall.

In all these towns the £10 householder was
to have a vote.

In the counties the representation had been a representation of freeholders only. The vote was to be continued to these freeholders ; but copyholders to the value of £10, liable to serve on juries were also to be permitted to vote ; and leaseholders, whose lease was for at least twenty-one years and had not been renewed within two years, were also to have the right of voting. The Isle of Wight was to have a county member. Yorkshire, the only county with four members, was now to have six, and twenty-six other counties which had previously had two members were now to be divided into districts and to have four.

In Scotland, as in England, the borough franchise was to be in the occupiers of houses rented or rated at not less than £10 a year. In the counties a beneficial interest in land or houses to the amount of £10 a year, in the nature of freehold or copyhold, or a lease by an occupier for at least nineteen years at £50 per annum, would confer the right of voting. The Scotch members had hitherto numbered forty-five. The seats were now to be redistributed so as to give the great towns, Edinburgh and Glasgow, two members instead of one, while five new members were distributed between the hitherto unrepresented towns, Aberdeen, Paisley, Dundee, Greenock, and Leith. In Ireland, although the intentions of the Ministry were originally as generous as they were in regard to the rest of the Kingdom, the county representation was left practically unaltered ; but a member was given to Belfast, Limerick, and Waterford. In Wales, one new district of boroughs (the Swansea district) was added, and to the old districts new towns were added. Proposals were added for the registration of votes, and for lessening the expense of elections by shortening the duration of the poll and increasing the number of polling places.

The result of these proposals was to abolish 168 seats and to create 106 new ones, and thus to diminish the total number of seats by sixty-two, the normal number being 658. It was anticipated that there would be added to the old borough constituencies 110,000 new votes, that there would be enfranchised in the new English boroughs 50,000, that 60,000 would be added to the Scotch electorate, that there would be 40,000 new borough voters, and that in the English counties there would be an increase of 100,000 electors, making a total estimated increase of half-a-million voters.

The Reformers, many of whom had given up all hope of getting any satisfactory measure from Government without a revolution, which, indeed, some of them were quite prepared to see very soon, were taken by surprise at the extent of the measure. The news of the bill spread like wild-fire through all the coffee-houses before Lord John Russell had long finished his speech, and when next day the newspapers confirmed the tidings there was general rejoicing. Though some of the Reformers got up a meeting to demand shorter parliaments and the ballot, this was not meant, according to the confession of Francis Place, one of its promoters, to be a serious demonstration. Their shrewd intention was to

make surer of the unexpected concessions
already made by demanding more. The idea
was that this would strengthen the hands of the
ministers if they were loyal to the people, while
it would perhaps warn them against retrogression
if they had any intention of allowing the Opposition to fritter away the provisions of so valuable
a measure. But no matter what the intention
of the promoters was, the meeting frustrated it.
The people, whatever measure they might have
preferred, were disposed to thank ministers for
what had been offered, and they knew well
the difficulty there would be in carrying such
a proposal. They were persuaded that the best
way to insure the success of the measure was to
oppose a unanimous front to the Tories, whose
ranks had been disorganised since the Duke of
Wellington's downfall, but were now again closing
in the face of this strong measure of reform.
Accordingly "unanimity" was adopted as the
popular watchword, and the petition for the
ballot and short parliaments was for the moment
thrown to the winds.

Adequately to appreciate the enormous importance of this proposed addition of half a million votes to the electorate, we must have clearly in mind the utter rottenness of the existing plan of representation. The *Spectator* analysed the House of Commons in that year, and showed that 175 members were actually returned on the nomination or under the patronage of 89 peers, while 100 more obtained their seats through the influence of 66 of their fellow members. The Government had direct possession of at least 9 seats. The Scotch borough members were returned by corporations which were described by Lord John Russell as self-elected. In the Scotch counties, the Dukes of Argyll and Buccleuch, the Earl of Hopetown and Mr. Maule had some influence, but, said the *Spectator*, " Bating the local and limited influence of a few such men, nearly all the boroughs, and, with a few exceptions, the whole of the counties of Scotland belong to the minister, or we should say to the ministry, rather than to any individual or set of individuals. No Government that has remained long in power has ever found the electors its opponents, and no party that has long remained out of power has ever found them its supporters. The system is one of open and undisguised bribery; but it is bribery not of money solely or even chiefly. The return for a vote is made, not in a few pounds, which an uncalculating and spendthrift elector proceeds to dissipate in a fortnight's rioting—it comes in the shape of an ensigncy for my son Tom, a situation in the customs for my brother Alexander, or a kirk it may be for my nephew James. The payment is one which only 'the powers that be' can make, and for that reason the powers that be, whether for good or for evil, have always commanded the elections. So steadily and universally has this influence been acted on that up to the period when Sir Robert Peel took to himself the patronage of Scotland (since which time it has been managed with the externals of decency), there was not an officer in that Kingdom, from the Lord President of the Court of Session, down to the tide-waiter of £30 a year, that did not derive his honours from his own or his friends' influence in some town council or county."

To illustrate the vices of the nomination system, one proprietor of Old Sarum had threatened to send his footman to represent that place in Parliament. At Beeralston, which, like Old Sarum, was one of the boroughs the bill proposed to disfranchise, only the returning officer and his clerk attended the election, which was a mere matter of form. Weobly, another doomed borough, belonged to the Marquis of Bath. Some of his servants were sent down a few days before the election, taking their beds with them. The right of returning members belonged in this borough to "the inhabitants of the ancient vote-houses." The servants of the Marquis having taken up their habitation in these houses for a day or two, duly returned his lordship's nominees on the day of election. Ludgershall was another borough returning its two members. Most of the houses there were ruins, but a doorway gave the right of voting. Gatton had once been sold to satisfy the

demands of the proprietor's creditors. Sir
Mark Wood, who bought it, had returned
himself as one of the members, and till his
death had regularly sold the other seat at
prices varying from £3,500 to £5,000. Sum-
ming up the whole matter almost in the words
of the contemporary authority already quoted,
it may be said generally, that where the suffrage
was confined to burgage holds, the real property
of the place was acquired by wealthy individuals
who conferred on friends, relations, or depend-
ents, the right of property during the period
of election. If the corporation had the right
of election, the influence of the neighbouring landed proprietor was often sufficient to
secure that its members, whose trade perhaps
depended on his goodwill, should yield him
practically the patronage of the borough.
Where the freemen shared in the vote, the
freedom of a borough was seldom conferred on
any individual on whose support the influential
landowner could not depend, and if any ventured
upon a course of independence, the pliant

majority were ready to create new freemen for the express purpose of turning the election. In many places, where the right of election had extended to the inhabitants paying scot and lot, the right of persons unfavourable to the man of influence was successfully defeated by omitting to rate them to pay the parish taxes. In the open boroughs money was expended in every kind of bribery. In some places juntos of individuals possessing great influence sold the borough for the highest sum they could get, and secured the votes by judiciously distributing among the people a small portion of the price thus obtained.

Such was the state of the representation against which the people, driven by the increasing pressure of taxation and other evils which they attributed to misgovernment, were at last protesting with irresistible earnestness. The bill of 1831 went far to abolish the defects of which they complained, and being determined to give no excuse for the withdrawal of such an unexpected boon, they impressed upon each other the necessity for the subordination of all more extreme demands. Their champion, Orator Hunt, attempted to talk to them of the ballot. This had hitherto been a pet scheme with them. But now they impatiently cried " Keep that for another time," and their watchword went forth, " The Bill, the whole Bill, and nothing but the Bill ! "

The sixty boroughs returning two members, which it was originally proposed to disfranchise by the bill of 1831, are given below, with the number of nominal electors as supplied for a Parliamentary return during the Reform Debates. The list should be read in connection with explanations given in the text, as to the manner in which these votes were subjected in nearly every case to the influence of the so-called proprietors of the borough, or of the bribery of borough-mongers. The boroughs which were afterwards saved from total extinction by the first Reform Act, are distinguished by an asterisk :—

Aldborough (York), about 80 electors, inhabitants paying
    scot and lot.
Aldeburgh (Suffolk), about 65 electors, freemen at large.
Appleby (Westmoreland), about 100 electors, burgage
    holders.

Bedwin (Wilts.), about 140 electors, freeholders and burgage holders.

Beeralston (Devon), about 30 electors, burgage holders.

Bishopscastle (Shropshire), about 190 electors, residents
for twelve months.

Bletchingley (Surrey), about 70 electors, burgage holders.

Bossiney (Cornwall), about 25 electors, burgess freeholders
resident.

Brackley (Northamptonshire), 33 electors, members of
corporation.

Bramber (Sussex), 17 electors, inhabitants of ancient
houses, or houses on ancient foundations.

* Buckingham, 13 electors, bailiff and burgesses.

Callington (Cornwall), 225 electors, freeholders and resident life leaseholders.

Camelford (Cornwall), 27 electors, free inhabitant burgesses paying scot and lot.

Castlerising, 50 electors, burgage tenement owners.

Corfe Castle (Dorsetshire), 278 electors, freeholders.

Dunwich (Suffolk), 33 electors, freemen.

* Eye, 125 electors, freemen.

Fowey (Cornwall), 320 electors, burgage tenement holders,
and scot and lot.

Gatton (Surrey), 7 electors, freeholders, and scot and lot
payers.

Haslemere (Surrey), 130 electors, resident freeholders.

Heyden (York), 410 electors, burgesses.

Heytesbury (Wilts), 26 electors, burgage tenement holders.

Higham Ferrers (Northampton), 33 electors, mayor, alder-
men, burgesses and freemen.

Hindon (Wilts), 170 electors, inhabitant householders, being parishioners.

Ilchester (Somerset), 200 electors, inhabitant householders.

Looe, East (Cornwall), 38 electors, capital and free burgesses.

Looe, West (Cornwall), 19 electors, capital and free burgesses, being residents.

Lostwithiel (Cornwall), 24 electors, corporation.

Ludgershall (Wilts), 150 electors, estates of inheritance, freehold or life lease.

* Malmesbury (Wilts), 13 electors, capital burgesses.

* Midhurst (Sussex), 41 electors, burgage tenants.

Milborne Port (Somerset), 311 electors, scot and lot payers.

Minehead (Somerset), 215 electors, housekeepers.

Newport (Cornwall), 70 electors, freeholders of ancient tenements, or sites thereof, and their rated occupiers.

Newton (Lancashire), 52 electors, freeholders or lifeholders.

Newton, or Frankville (Isle of Wight), 31 electors, mayor, and burgesses.

Okehampton (Devon), 230 electors, freemen and freeholders.

Orford (Suffolk), 22 electors, mayor, portmen, capital burgesses, and freemen.

* Petersfield (Hampshire), 36 electors, freeholders.

Plympton (Devon), 54 electors, freemen.

Queenborough (Kent), 315 electors, eldest sons of freemen born, or apprentices to a resident freeman for seven years.

* Reigate (Surrey), 59 electors, burgage tenants and free holders.

Romney (Kent), 21 electors, freemen.

St. Mawes (Cornwall), 87 electors, householders and free-holders.

St. Michael's (Cornwall), 7 electors, portreeve and in-habitants.

Saltash (Cornwall), 154 electors, burgage tenants.

Sarum, Old (Wilts.), 13 electors, burgage tenure.

Seaford (Sussex), 96 electors, housekeepers paying scot and lot.

Steyning (Sussex,) 118 electors, scot and lot payers.

Stockbridge (Hampshire), 150 electors, housekeepers pay-ing scot and lot.

Tregony (Cornwall), 265 electors, all persons boiling a pot except paupers.

* Wareham (Dorsetshire), 218 electors, scot and lot payers.

Wendover (Bucks), about 140 electors, inhabitant house-holders.

Weobly (Herefordshire), 93 electors, inhabitants of ancient vote-houses.

Whitchurch (Hampshire), 37 electors, freeholders.

Winchelsea (Sussex), 10 electors, those elected by the body corporate.

* Woodstock (Oxford), about 164 electors, mayor, alder-men and freemen.

Wootton Bassett (Wilts), 198 electors, householders pay-ing scot and lot.

Yarmouth (I. W.), 11 electors, mayor and burgesses

CHAPTER VIII.

THE STRUGGLE OF 1831—2. THE FIRST REFORM ACT.

NOTWITHSTANDING the enthusiasm of the people, the Bill of 1831 encountered obstinate resistance from the House of Commons. The debate on its introduction lasted for seven nights, and consisted of no fewer than seventy-one speeches. The opposition was founded chiefly on a denial of the right to disfranchise the boroughs, on the fear of Republicanism, and on the alleged tendency of the Bill to set class against class. The abolition of the close boroughs was denounced as Corporation robbery, and Sir Robert Peel defended the boroughs as having been the means of gaining admission to the House of many of its most famous members, and of retaining their abilities for the benefit

of the House and the country, when election
accidents had deprived them of seats elsewhere.
Sir Robert was not slow to avail himself of the
argument that the £10 franchise would actually
deprive some voters of the suffrage, and he censured the Government for agitating this question
at such a crisis.   Hunt and O'Connell maintained
the right of the people to a still larger measure of Reform, but their voices had little weight,
for the same reason as that which induced the
people out of doors to support the Bill as it
stood.   When the Bill was at length introduced,
there was great rejoicing in the country, and
addresses of thanks were sent to the King.   The
debate on the second reading was most exciting
in its result, the majority being one vote in a
House of 603 members, and that one vote was
only obtained by the defection of a member of the
Opposition, who had held office under the Duke
of Wellington.   The Opposition regarded this
as tantamount to victory.   In the country it was
talked of as a great success for the Government,
considering that they had the whole force of the

borough-mongers to fight. The majority of one was therefore signalized in the great towns by illuminations and other indications of popular joy. Lord Grey wrote :—" The activity, the intrigue, the falsehood that was used to influence votes is not to be described. •What hurt us most was the report so industriously propagated that the King had put a positive veto on a proposal to dissolve the Parliament." This report, it seems, accurately represented what had happened. For two days before this division on the 18th of March, Lord Grey had been greatly annoyed by the defeat of a proposal for the reduction of the timber duties. He attributed this defeat to a combination of those whose interests were concerned with the enemies of Parliamentary Reform, and foreseeing the injury which this division would cause his Government, he had thought it well to get the King's opinion in advance on the subject of a dissolution. When His Majesty was approached on this question he was under the influence of annoyance at some recent free criticisms in the House of Commons on the civil list expenditure,

and was evidently beginning to rue his assent to
the Reform Bill, which he described to his Prime
Minister as a measure " which must have the
effect of giving a more popular character to the
House of Commons, and therefore the effect also
of increasing the disposition of its members to
oppose the influence of the people to that of
the Crown and the aristocracy." With these
feelings he point blank declined to agree to a
dissolution.

Between the second reading and the Committee stage Lord John Russell announced some
modifications in the Bill. The boroughs that
were to be abolished had been named in
schedule A of the Bill, while the boroughs to
be limited to one member were included in a
schedule marked B. Five out of the sixty
boroughs mentioned at the end of last chapter
were now taken out of schedule A and
transferred to schedule B. These were Aldborough, Buckingham, Reigate, Malmesbury,
Okehampton.

Eight were to be taken out of schedule B, and

eight additional counties were to have an extra member. To the newly enfranchised towns were to be added Oldham, Bury, Rochdale, Whitby Wakefield, Salford, Stoke-on-Trent, each returning one member. The number of members was thus reduced by only 34, instead of 64 as originally contemplated. With regard to the right of voting the sons of freemen born before the introduction of the Bill, and apprentices indentured before the same date, were to enjoy the electoral privilege on coming of age or taking out their freedom. The modifications failed to satisfy the opponents of the Bill, and a great fight took place upon the motion of General Gascoyne against the diminution of members for England. Exception was taken then as it is taken to-day to the aggrandisement of the Irish and Scotch at the expense of the English representation. Mr. Stanley met this argument with the following warning: "I caution hon. members who stickle so pertinaciously for the maintenance of the proportion of members between the three countries, and who grudge to Ireland any increase of

representatives beyond the number given to her
at the period of the Union, to consider well the
arguments which they are thus putting into the
hands of those who are contending for a measure
which I conceive would be most mischievous
both to England and Ireland—I mean the repeal
of the Union—and who put forward the doctrine
that Ireland is not adequately represented in
this House, and is therefore entitled to have a
domestic legislature of her own. . . . . If we
are to have a United Parliament, we ought not
to adhere too strictly to the existing scale of
proportion between the representatives of the
three Kingdoms." O'Connell pointed out the
great number of new town representatives given
to England as compared with Ireland ; and
maintained that there were 14 towns in his
country which would have been enfranchised
had they been in England.

All interest in the argument of this debate
was eclipsed by the excitement involved in its
result, which was the defeat of the Government
by 8 votes, the numbers being 299 to 291.

The Cabinet, notwithstanding the King's previous expression of opinion, insisted upon advising dissolution ; and the King not only gave way, but in order to assist the Ministry in thwarting the tactics of the Opposition in the Lords, who were about to adopt an address to His Majesty, praying him not to dissolve, agreed to go down suddenly, and threatened to go in a hackney coach if the ordinary retinue were not at once available. The delight of the populace, when it became known that the King had prorogued Parliament, found expression in fresh illuminations, in feasting, and in meetings innumerable. The elections that followed were fierce. " Report," said the *Morning Chronicle,* " makes the sums subscribed by the Tories enormous. We have heard of £400,000 to £500,000, and of the Duke of Northumberland alone subscribing £100,000. We should think there was exaggeration in this ; but the borough-mongers are fighting for their freeholds." They fought in vain, however, against the efforts of an excited and enthusiastic people.

A Parliamentary Candidate Society was started
to provide members for reforming constituencies ;
a " Loyal and Patriotic Fund for Reform " was
subscribed, and the people won the day. At
Dover, a nomination borough under the influence
of the Duke of Wellington, a Tory was turned
out.   General Gascoyne, the author of the
Government defeat, was thrust out of Liverpool ;
Sir Richard Vyvyan, who had moved the rejection of the Bill on the second reading, lost his
seat in Cornwall. A reformer who had committed the indiscretion of voting with General
Gascoyne, was turned out of Southwark. Nearly
all the counties and open boroughs returned
members pledged to support the Bill.

In the meantime, the King referred to the
Bill as a fearful experiment, and kept urging
Earl Grey to alter the measure so as to avoid
conflict with the Lords ; but Lord Grey firmly
replied that no concession was possible in the
face of the strong current of public opinion.
Upon the re-assembling of Parliament, therefore,
the Bill was reintroduced. Lord John Russell

paid a high tribute to the conduct of the people, stating that in the sacrifices made, and the devotedness shown by the humbler classes of the community in the pursuit of what they thought was their duty to their country, they had set an example of which England might well be proud to the latest generations. The Bill as re-introduced added the two boroughs of Down-ton and St. Germains to the boroughs to be disfranchised. On the 7th of July, after three nights' discussion, it was read a second time by 367 to 231, a majority of 136. After this, the Anti-Reformers could only oppose to the Bill the tactics of delay; and the measure was ob-structed by prolonged fights, varied by motions for adjournment upon the question of the dis-franchisement of each rotten borough separately.

The Chandos clause was first heard of and carried in these debates in committee. The Marquis of Chandos was of opinion that the clause extending the county franchise to £50 leaseholders should also be granted to tenants at will of holdings having the same value. It was objected to the proposition that the tenants would not be sufficiently independent and would vote as they were told by their landlords, but in the end the Marquis of Chandos carried the day by 84 votes.

The bill was in committee from the 12th July to 15th September. Its third reading was carried by 113 to 58, and finally the motion that the bill do pass was adopted by 345 to 236, a majority of 109.

The long delay in the House of Commons had irritated the people, who suspected Ministers for want of loyalty to the measure, owing to their failure to push it through more rapidly, and they awaited somewhat sullenly, or at all events with damped spirits, the progress of events. But when the bill was approaching the close of its House of Commons career, the people determined to show the House that their desire to have the Bill had by no means abated. In answer to the insinuation that the public feeling had subsided, meetings were held afresh and the political unions, whose influence increased as the struggle grew fiercer, became most active, with a view to convincing the House of Lords of their continued desire for the Bill. At a meeting in the City, Col. Torrens, M.P., wound up a speech in which, discussing the wide-spread question, What will the Lords do? he concluded with the following passage to illustrate what would be done with them if they thwarted the will of the nation :—

" The story of the Sybil will be remembered. She brought her mystic leaves to the high authorities of Rome and demanded a high price. She was refused. She took half the leaves away, and returning, again demanded her price, and was again refused. The leaves were again reduced one half, and she came again and demanded her price, when the authorities became alarmed and they gave her her price. Now, gentlemen, we will a little reverse the story. We come to them with this bill, and nothing but this bill. If they reject it we will come to them again and demand something more. If they again reject it, we will come again with a bill in which the House of Lords shall be inserted in Schedule A."

The Bill was recommended to the Peers in a touching speech by Earl Grey, who towards the close of his oration administered a solemn warning to the Bishops, to reflect what their situation would be if by their votes the Bill should be thrown out. The debate on the second reading lasted five days, and towards its close the Lord Chancellor adopted Col. Torrens' reference to the Sybil, and clothing it in more eloquent language, heightened the effect of the warning to his fellow Peers. The warning, however, was unheeded. At 6 o'clock on the morning of the 8th Oct., the Bill was thrown out by 199 votes against 158, the majority against the Bill thus being forty-one.

When this news reached Birmingham, funeral bells were tolled from the churches and chapels. Meetings were held all over the metropolis. The merchants and the bankers met at the Mansion House to approve the Bill, and to ask the King to continue his Ministers, and create new Peers. The House of Commons passed a vote of confidence in the Ministers. A remarkable demonstration was made at Birmingham, where an open-air meeting was called, which was attended by over 100,000 people. And now, while the correspondence was actually going on between the King and Earl Grey, relative to the King's regret that no concession had been made to the Peers, the multitude assembled at Birmingham were applauding the statement of Atwood, their chairman, that to the King personally they owed more in this great work of Reform than to any other human being in existence. "All of you take off your hats," he said, "look up to the heavens, where the just God rules both heavens and earth, and cry out, with one heart and with one voice, God bless the King." "Every head," says a contemporary report, "was bared, every face was turned up to heaven, and at one moment, 100,000 voices answered to the exhortation—'God bless the King!'"

At a great meeting at Regent's Park, in London, much exasperation was exhibited against the Bishops, and a resolution was passed which was afterwards published in a mourning border, declaring that while the meeting would wait with patience, and therefore pay the public taxes, until the Ministers should have time to adopt the necessary measures to secure the passing of the Reform Bill, it was their unalterable resolution, if an anti-Reform and Tory Administration should take the place of Earl Grey and his colleagues, to withold the payment of tithes and taxes. An imposing procession of the working classes of London was arranged about this time, in which it was said that 300,000 men took part. Francis Place, from whose manuscript records many of these details are obtained, says that in all the shops of Marylebone there were placards with the words " The King, Liberty, and Reform," and he tells how the members of the procession punished persons who by riotous conduct were likely to bring discredit upon their demonstration. Though these precautions did not save some distinguished peers from rough usage at the hands of the people, the Reformers took credit to themselves for preserving the peace generally by the agency of these organized Political Unions, upon whose members patience was strongly urged at this crisis, and it was pointed out that at Derby and Nottingham, where serious riots took place, no Unions had at that time been formed. Upon the news of the rejection of the 'Reform Bill arriving at these places, the people became so tumultuous and so angry in their demonstrations against anti-Reformers, that soldiers had to be brought into the towns to subdue them. In Derby, the mob attacked the gaol in which some of their number had been placed, and set the prisoners free. At Nottingham, more tragical scenes were enacted. Several properties were destroyed, and the burning of Nottingham Castle marked in tragic manner the popular hate of the Duke of Newcastle, one of the most thorough-going opponents of the Bill. There was a Political Union at Bristol, where a few weeks later riots of a still more alarming character, involving the loss of many lives, took place. But the Reformers resented the notion that they had any responsibility for the dreadful scenes which have given that city an evil distinction in our history. They even accused members of the corporation of desiring to see a good Bristol riot, which might prejudice the cause of Reform. The corporation there did not represent the citizens, and could not always maintain the public peace. They were justly apprehensive that when Sir Charles Wetherill, their Recorder, came to the city to discharge his judical duties, he would meet with a warm reception from the multitude on account of the activity of his hostility to the Reform Bill. The Recorder was detested by the Reformers, who regarded him as their "bitter and unrelenting enemy." Accordingly, efforts were made to get Sir C. Wetherill to postpone his visit ; these failing, the magistrates had arranged to have troops in readiness. The Political Union of that city was too much irritated at this proceeding to promise their active aid in maintaining public peace. They expressed the opinion, that if the magistrates

were incompetent to preserve the peace without
the military, they should resign their offices.
At the same time members of the Union and
Reformers generally were "recommended at all
times of popular excitement to use their most
strenuous endeavours for the preservation of
the public peace, as it is only by such a course
they will obtain the reforms they seek." How
Sir Charles Wetherill was received at Bristol,
how a violent Bristol mob attacked the public
buildings he entered, how he had to make
his escape in disguise after an ignominious
scramble across the roofs of houses, how, by the
mismanagement of the municipal authorities and
the indecisive conduct of the troops, the rioting
grew fiercer till building after building was
demolished and fired, the palace of the Bishop
of Bath and Wells (an opponent of the Bill)
sacrificed to the flames, and the rioters eventually only dispersed after terrible bloodshed—
all this is matter of general history, needing
to be recalled only to exemplify the excitement
prevailing in the country, after the refusal of the

Lords to pass the **Reform Bill.** The hostility to the Bishops was manifested in many other towns besides Bristol. Prelates were burned in effigy, the Archbishop of Canterbury (Dr. Howley) was publicly spat upon, and a suggestion that Canterbury Cathedral should be turned into a cavalry stable was actually greeted at a public meeting with applause.

Before these occurrences at Bristol, the Parliament had been prorogued, with those assurances of future intentions with regard to the Bill without which the whole country would probably have been in a blaze. For between the rejection of the Bill and the prorogation there had been a rapid growth of impatience with Ministers. Why did they not get the King to prorogue Parliament at once, to create new peers, and assemble the Houses again in a few days to pass the bill? One deputation bearded Earl Grey in his house at nearly midnight to urge him to get all this done within seven days. His reply, or rather the rumours of its purport, excited further impatience. It was feared that

Parliament would not be again convened till after Christmas, and that the Bill would be altered to suit the dissenting Peers. All the while, however, Earl Grey had been pressing on the King, in spite of his alarms at the outrages in the country, the indispensable necessity of giving the Royal sanction to the submission of a new measure, founded on the same principles as the rejected Bill, and of equal efficacy for the correction of the defects in the representation. After the prorogation he continued to soothe the King's fear of the popular agitation, and while His Majesty expressed hopes that those whom he called the promoters of mischief and violence would " eventually so commit themselves as to justify their arrest," the Prime Minister did not fail to point out that the organizations so suspected by the King had received a great impulse and extension from the rejection of the Reform Bill, and to tell him plainly that if the Bill were again to fail he could not be answerable for the public peace. By and by the effect of the circulation of rumours that the King might dismiss his Ministers, and call the Tories back to power, justified Lord Grey's predictions. The people began to talk of their rights, under Magna Charta, to possess arms for their self defence. The Duke of Wellington alarmed the King with an intimation that a contract had been entered into for the supply of arms to the Political Union of Birmingham, and Earl Grey was again involved in a difficult correspondence with the King. In his letters, however, he pointed out the absence of proof of any proposed organization of an armed force, and boldly reminded his sovereign that the privilege of having and using arms was reserved to Englishmen by the constitution, and that if members of Unions merely resolved to have arms individually, without being formed or organised as armed bodies, he knew of no authority under the existing law, by which they could be prevented. Lord Grey, however, could not deny that a proposition which soon afterwards emanated from Birmingham, to constitute a body which practically usurped the functions of local government, was illegal; and a proclamation was issued, warning the public against connecting themselves with such associations. The Union at Birmingham, however, had been warned before the proclamation was issued of the illegal character of the proposed organization, and had abandoned it. The Political Unions on the ordinary basis maintained that the proclamation did not affect them, and continued their proceedings undisturbed.

The King now devoted himself to preparation for the coming crisis in the Lords, and, warned by his Ministers of the danger of another check to the Reform Bill, lent active assistance in the endeavour to bring matters to a peaceable issue. With this view he encouraged communications between a number of Tory peers, afterwards known as the waverers, and himself, endeavoured by means of attentions shown to the Archbishop of Canterbury to secure a more conciliatory attitude on the part of the Bishops. The waverers, of whom Lord Wharncliffe was the

chief, had at last come to the conclusion that
the rotten boroughs must go, but did not make
their reluctant admission until they had forced
from the Ministry certain concessions which led
to the reopening of the Reform question much
sooner in after years than might have been
expected. Lord Grey would give way neither to
the Opposition nor to the King in regard to the
proposed new metropolitan boroughs which they
desired him to throw into the county divisions.
But to soothe their fears, the Prime Minister
agreed to insert a provision limiting the right of
voting under the £10 franchise to those who
were actually rated on their own account. The
express object of this was to limit the numbers
voting in large constituencies. Lord Grey also
conceded a reduction of the number of towns to
be limited to one member and agreed to transfer
certain towns to Schedule B (towns with one
member) which had previously been put in
Schedule A as boroughs to be disfranchised. In
this way, Midhurst, Petersfield, Eye, Wareham,
and Woodstock were saved from disfranchise-

ment. The number of members he agreed should remain at 658, as originally contended for when the Bill met with its first check in the Commons. This altered the proportions of members given to Ireland, for the spare representatives were given to English towns and to Monmouth, but none to the sister country. In fact the King commended this redistribution on the express ground that it would shut out the claim of Ireland to more members. The boroughs to be disfranchised were to be selected according to the number of houses rather than to population, and certain ancient rights of franchise were preserved to residents.

The meeting of parliament on the 6th December was reassuring to the excited public. Though the Irish members were furious at their treatment and the more ardent Radicals regarded the alterations in the Bill as blemishes, the fiery opposition of Sir R. Peel and his friends and the anxiety to pass the Bill through the House of Lords secured the Government the continued support of the country. The Bill got into committee after the Christmas recess by 152 votes to 99, and, soon after, the decayed boroughs were swept away by 198 votes to 123. The Chandos clause had been incorporated in the new Bill and it was now re-debated. The opponents of the clause reiterated the objection that the yearly tenants would not be independent but would vote at the bidding of their landlords, and maintained that the effect of passing the clause would simply be to create certain nomination counties. The Chandos qualification, however, was maintained by 272 votes against 32. A strong protest was made by some members, without avail, against making payment of rent or rate any condition of the franchise. One of the stiffest fights was on the subject of the metropolitan representation. The Marquis of Chandos, maintaining that the new members to the London boroughs would give the capital a predominating influence, proposed an amendment with the object of merging them in Southwark and Westminster, instead of giving them special representation. The Ministers triumphed over this amendment by a majority of 80—316 to 236. The Bill passed its third reading by a majority of 116, and on March 26th, 1832, was carried to the Lords. Here the Government had ample warning of the difficulties in store for them. The waverers in intimating their intention to vote for the second reading demanded as the condition of their further support that extensive alterations should be conceded in committee. Thus, although the second reading was obtained by a majority of nine (184—175) there was no confidence either on the part of the Government or of the people that the Bill would be passed. The only hope the people had was in an extensive creation of Peers. For this there had been a general demand for some time, and indeed it had been a subject of communications between the King and the Cabinet more than once during the previous three or four months. In fact, but for the threat of an addition to the House of Lords the Bill would not have proceeded so far as it had done. Only the strong objections of William IV. to any ex-

tensive creation of Peers had induced the Cabinet
to refrain from insisting upon this measure being
taken, even before the second reading.   But the
Chancellor of the Exchequer had threatened to
resign if Peers were not created, other members
of the Cabinet sympathised with his views, and
it was intimated to His Majesty that in the
event of the Bill being rejected on the second
reading they would propose the alternative of
their resignation or the immediate prorogation
of Parliament and such addition to the House
of Lords as would afford a certainty of success.
When the King in an interview at Windsor,
hinted to Lord Grey, that it might be possible
to effect some compromise and embody it in a
new Bill, this elicited from Lord Grey a strong
representation to the effect, as stated by the
Prime Minister in his own memorandum of
the conversation, " That the public impatience
would neither wait for such a negotiation nor
accept from the present Ministers, and probably
not from any others, what would bear the
character of a mutilated measure; that I could

not, without entirely disqualifying myself from acting usefully for His Majesty's service propose anything which would be so entirely at variance with all the declarations which I have made on this subject ; that I was afraid the evil would not stop here and that if there should be any delay in taking the measures which appeared to be necessary to obviate the effects of the general disappointment, the consequence would be that instead of waiting with a disposition to accept a modified plan of Reform there would be a renewed cry for universal suffrage and the vote by ballot which had ceased since the present measure was proposed." The King was induced to contemplate the creation of a reasonable number of Peers, but evidently did so with the extremest reluctance, and with reservations which were not calculated to increase the confidence of the Cabinet.

In the country of course it was not known what was taking place in the Cabinet, and as the rumour was circulated that the King would not create Peers, there was no little excitement

during the Easter recess. The meetings promoted by the Unions were resumed, and from
the great towns addresses were sent to the King,
imploring him to have recourse to a fearless and
liberal exercise of his royal prerogative in the
creation of Peers. A gigantic demonstration
was made at Birmingham, where some 200,000
persons—members of the Birmingham Union,
and the Unions of adjacent towns—assembled at
Newhall Hill, to convince the Lords that they
had not ceased to care for the Bill, and to
petition them in its favour. The earnestness of
this vast assembly found expression in this
solemn vow which, with heads uncovered, the
people repeated after one of the speakers—

"WITH UNBROKEN FAITH, THROUGH EVERY
PERIL AND PRIVATION, WE HERE DEVOTE
OURSELVES AND OUR CHILDREN TO OUR
COUNTRY'S CAUSE."

The Hymn of the Unions, sung on the same
occasion, testified to the fervour of the populace :—

God is our guide ! from field, from wave,
  From plough, from anvil, and from loom,
We come our country's rights to save,
  And speak a tyrant faction's doom ;
And hark ! we raise from sea to sea,
  The sacred watchword, Liberty.

God is our guide ! no swords we draw,
  We kindle not war's battle fires ;
By union, justice, reason, law,
  We claim the birthright of our sires ;
We raise the watchword, Liberty,
  We will, we will, we will be free !

On the reassembling of the House of Lords, the tactics of the Opposition were indicated by Lord Lyndhurst's motion (May 7th), that the consideration of the disfranchisement clauses should be postponed till after the enfranchising clauses had been gone over. Lord Grey resisted this indirect attack, and was defeated by 151—116. The next day the Cabinet called upon His Majesty to create new Peers, or accept their resignation, and His Majesty, alarmed at the number of Peers demanded, accepted the resignation.

The announcement that Ministers had . resigned, came like a thunderbolt on the country. An appalling. crisis ensued. The membership of the Unions increased by thousands every day, and their meetings were marked by the greatest excitement.

The Common Council of London passed resolutions declaring those who advised His Majesty's resistance to be the enemies of their Sovereign, and urging the people to petition Parliament to withhold the supplies. The Livery lifted their voice in the same strain ; the name of the Queen, whose influence was supposed to have been at work, was received with groans and hisses by the electors of Westminster. Immense cheering greeted a reference of O'Connell's to the fate which overtook Charles I. who dared to listen to the advice of his foreign wife. The "Sailor King" was no longer the hero of the crowd, but was actually insulted in the streets, while Colonel Jones could say of him with impunity, and even with approbation, that "if William IV. pursued with lamentable obsti-

nacy an evil course, whether at the instance of
the woman of his bosom, or of the creatures of
his Court, or if he placed himself in the hands of
his unpopular Duke of Cumberland ; in a word,
if he forgot the people, the people should forget
him." At Birmingham, placards were placed in
the shop windows, bearing the following inscrip-
tion :—

NOTICE.

NO TAXES PAID HERE

UNTIL

THE REFORM BILL IS PASSED.

Another great meeting was held at Newhall
Hill, and a petition was adopted to Parliament,
in which occurred an ominous reference to the
right of the people to arm in their own defence.
On the 10th, the House of Commons immediately
voted an address to the King imploring him to
call to his counsels only such as would carry
into effect the Reform Bill, unimpaired in all its
essential provisions. It was evident that no
Ministry could exist that did not take up the

question of Reform ; and the Duke of Wellington actually undertook to form a Ministry on this understanding. Naturally, the announcement created intense indignation. It was declared that the people would not have their rights from such a polluted source ; and in the House of Commons the indignation expressed was so strong and so general as to render it impossible for the Duke to persevere in the attempt to form a Ministry. There was nothing for it but to recall Earl Grey, and to face the dreaded prospect of a creation of Peers. To avoid this painful necessity, however, the King resolved on an extraordinary step. He allowed intimations to be given to certain Peers that this measure would have to be resorted to unless they stayed away. The knowledge that Lord Grey had the King's authority to create Peers in his pocket had the desired effect on the stubborn peers. The course taken by His Majesty removed all obstacles to the procedure of the Bill, which, with the Irish and Scotch measures, was speedily passed, not without some expressions of disappointment and surprise from the King himself that the measures were passing so rapidly and with so little alteration. The Bills soon became law ; but the royal assent was given by commission. Nothing could induce His Majesty to crown the success of such measures by performing this ceremony in person.

———— ——   ——————

A summary of the principal changes made by the Reform Acts of 1832 is appended :—

ENGLAND AND WALES—500 MEMBERS.

Fifty-six Boroughs totally disfranchised.

Old Sarum, Newtown (I.W.), St. Michael's *or* Midshall, Gatton, Bramber, Bossiney, Dunwich, Ludgershall, St. Mawe's, Beeralston, West Looe, St. Germain's, Newport, Blechingley, Aldborough, Camelford, Heyden, East Looe, Corfe Castle, Great Bedwin, Yarmouth (Isle of Wight), Queenborough, Castle Rising, East Grinstead, Higham Ferrers, Wendover, Weobly, Winchilsea, Tregony, Haslemere, Saltash, Orford, Callington, Newton, Ilchester, Boroughbridge, Stockbridge, New Romney, Hindon, Plympton, Seaford, Heytesbury, Steyning, Whitchurch, Wootton Bassett, Downton, Fowey, Milborne Port, Aldeburgh, Minehead, Bishop's Castle, Okehampton, Appleby, Lostwithiel, Brackley, and Amersham.

One Borough left with two instead of four Members.

Weymouth.

Thirty Boroughs left with one Member.

Petersfield, Ashburton, Eye, Westbury, Wareham, Midhurst, Woodstock, Wilton, Malmesbury, Liskeard, Reigate, Hythe, Droitwich, Lyme Regis, Launceston, Shaftesbury, Thirsk, Christchurch, Horsham, Great Grimsby, Calne, Arundel, St. Ives, Rye, Clitheroe, Morpeth, Helston, Northallerton, Wallingford, and Dartmouth.

The New Parliamentary Boroughs.

Twenty-two sending two Members.—Manchester, Birmingham, Leeds, Greenwich, Sheffield, Sunderland, Devonport, Wolverhampton, Tower Hamlets, Finsbury, Marylebone, Lambeth, Bolton, Bradford, Blackburn, Brighton, Halifax, Macclesfield, Oldham, Stockport, Stoke-upon-Trent, and Stroud.

Twenty sending one Member. — Ashton-under-Lyne, Bury, Chatham, Cheltenham, Dudley, Frome, Gateshead, Huddersfield, Kidderminster, Kendal, Rochdale, Salford, South Shields, Tynemouth, Wakefield, Walsall, Warrington, Whitby, Whitehaven, and Merthyr Tydvil.

Seven Counties entitled to send a third Member.

Berkshire, Buckinghamshire, Cambridgeshire, Dorsetshire, Herefordshire, Hertfordshire, and Oxfordshire.

Twenty-six Counties divided—each division sending two Members.

Cheshire, Cornwall, Cumberland, Derbyshire, Devonshire, Durham, Essex, Gloucestershire, Hampshire, Kent, Lancashire, Leicestershire, Lincolnshire, Norfolk, Northumberland, Northamptonshire, Nottinghamshire, Shropshire, Somersetshire, Staffordshire, Suffolk, Surrey, Sussex, Warwickshire, Wiltshire, Worcestershire.

New County (one Member).

Isle of Wight.

Additional Representation for Yorkshire.

Yorkshire entitled to send six members instead of four —two for each of the three Ridings.

Welsh Counties and Districts.

Caermarthen, Denbigh, and Glamorgan entitled to send two members instead of one. About 40 places entitled to share in the elections of the principal boroughs. Swansea district formed.

SCOTLAND— 53 MEMBERS.

Changes in the Burghs.

Edinburgh and Glasgow entitled to send second members; Aberdeen, Paisley, Dundee, Greenock, and Perth to have one member; Rothesay, Peebles, and Selkirk thrown into the counties. Sixty-nine towns formed into 14 districts of burghs, each sending one member. Total Burgh members, 23.

Changes in the Counties.

Elgin, combined with Nairn, Ross with Cromarty, and Clackmannan with Kinross, and portions of Perthshire and Stirlingshire. These combinations to return one member, making, with a member for each of 27 other counties, 30 county members.

IRELAND—105 MEMBERS.

Second members given to the town of Galway, to the cities of Limerick and Waterford, to the borough of Belfast, and the university of Dublin.

PERSONS ENTITLED TO VOTE UNDER THE REFORM ACTS OF 1832.

In *English Counties.* — 1. Forty shilling freeholders, being seised or possessed of inheritance; or being life-holders who came into possession before June, 1832, whether in actual possession or only in receipt of rents, or who, coming subsequently into possession, were in *bonâ fide* occupation, or had acquired their holdings by marriage, marriage settlement, devise, or promotion to any benefice or office. 2. £10 freeholders. 3. £10 copy-holders. 4. Tenants at a yearly rent of £50. 5. Lease-holders for 60 years at clear yearly value of £10. 6. Leaseholders for 20 years paying £50 clear yearly value. 7. Mortgagees in possession of freeholds, if after payment of interest there remained a clear yearly value of £10; or in actual possession and receipt of rents of the yearly value of 40s. 8. Leasehold mortgagees in

possession of yearly values of £10.   9.   Trustees in
receipt of requisite rents.   10.   Beneficed clergymen.
11.   Annuitants from freehold or copyhold, the latter
claim being registered 12 months prior to election.
12.   Holders of life-offices with emoluments (not less than
40*s.*) arisiug out of lands.   13.   Purchasers of redeemed
land tax (40*s.*).   14.   Irremovable schoolmasters, parish
clerks and sextons.   15.   Proprietors of tithes and rent-
charges (40*s.*).   16.   Joint tenants whose separate interests
amounted to 40*s.* freehold or £10 leasehold.   17.   Owners
of shares in mines, rivers, canals, fairs, markets, &c., if
amounting to an interest in the soil of sufficient annual
value.   *Note.*   No person could vote in a county in respect
of property that would confer on him a qualification to
vote for a borough ; but a freehold in a borough of the
annual value of 40*s.*, under £10, entitled the owner to a
vote for the county, and above £10 if in the occupation of
the tenant.   If he occupied it himself he had no county
vote.

In English Boroughs.—1.   The ancient franchise
holders in boroughs not disfranchised if their qualifications existed on the last day of July in the year for which
they claimed, and if they had resided for six months in
the borough or within 7 miles, and their names were on
the register.   2.   Occupiers either as owners or tenants of
any house, warehouse, or counting-house, shop, or other
building, *either with or without land,* of the clear yearly
value of £10 within the borough, provided they had been
in possession 12 calendar months prior to the last day of
July in the year of the claim and had paid before 20th July

all the poor-rates and assessed taxes payable from them in respect of the premises previous to the April preceding. 3. Lodgers if sharing with other lodgers and the value divided by number of lodgers came to £10 a year for each. If the landlord occupied any part of the house he, and not his lodgers, was in occupation.

In Scotch Counties.—The persons possessed of the suffrage before March, 1831, or who would have been entitled to it, that is to say, tenants in chief of the Crown with lands of 40 shillings (old extent), or of £400 Scotch valued rent, together with owners of land of £10 annual value ; 57 years leaseholders and life-holders with a clear £10 yearly interest, 19 years leaseholders with do., yearly tenants at a £50 rent, and all tenants whose interest had cost them £300.

In Scotch Cities, Burghs, and Contributory Districts.— The occupiers of houses of £10 clear yearly value, whether as proprietor, tenant, life-renter, or joint-occupier, with the non-resident true owners of similar premises, and husbands *jure uxoris* after the death of their wives holding by the courtesy of Scotland.

In Irish Counties.—£10 freeholders ; leaseholders for lives and copyholders of estates of £10 ; 60 years lease-holders and their assignees of estates of the same value ; 14 years leaseholders of £20 estates.

In Irish Cities and Boroughs.—£10 occupiers and resident freemen if by birth or servitude, or admitted before March, 1831.

CHAPTER IX.

FROM £10 FRANCHISE TO HOUSEHOLD SUFFRAGE.

HOW THE WHIGS WERE "DISHED."

LORD JOHN RUSSELL for some time bore
the nick-name of "Finality Jack" because of
his declarations that the 1832 Reform Act was
intended to be a settlement of the Reform
question. But the country never did accept
this Act as final. The limitations put on the
£10 franchise to satisfy the Tory peers and
quieten the fears of William IV., had the effect
in a very few years of raising fresh agitation.
The franchise in the counties was complained
of as having simply handed over the county
constituencies to the Tory party. A cry arose
for the Ballot. Both on that Reform and on
the abolition of Septennial Parliaments the
opinion of the legislature was repeatedly taken,

but without any favourable verdict.   The bogey always invoked by Ministers to frighten Parliament when these demands were made, was Universal Suffrage.   A stand must be made, it was said, or this frightful evil would be upon them.   The cry long served the ministerial purpose in Parliament; but outside St. Stephen's the demand for further Reform gathered strength, and took shape in the Chartist movement, which but for the mistakes of its leaders, must have proved irresistible, and which, as it was, undoubtedly convinced an unwilling legislature that the "finality" of the Act of 1832 was a dream.

The "six points" of the People's Charter were :—

1. Manhood Suffrage.
2. Annual Parliaments.
3. Vote by Ballot.
4. Abolition of the Property Qualification for Members of the House of Commons.
5. Payment of Members.
6. Equal Electoral Districts.

It was to O'Connell that the Charter owed its name. On Mr. Duncombe's failure to impress Parliament with the need for Reform in 1838, the minority who had voted with him co-operated with a committee of the London Working Men's Association, and drew up a bill embodying the above proposals. " There," said O'Connell to one of the working men representatives, when the labour was finished, " There is your Charter; agitate for it, and never be content with anything less." The working classes throughout the kingdom hailed the movement with enthusiasm, joined its ranks, supported its newspapers, and shouted for the six points at great torchlight meetings. Unfortunately for their own cause, the more desperate of the Chartists—men maddened by the miseries of their fellows at a time of social distress, such as was endured before the repeal of the Corn Laws—met the apathy of Parliament by threatening an appeal to force. A Methodist minister at Ashton-under-Lyne elicited a startling demonstration. Asking at a Chartist

N

meeting if the men had come armed, he was answered by the discharge of pistols into the air. Not satisfied with the first report he put a further question. The volley fired in response was a convincing answer to his question. The speaker coolly said : "I see it's all right ; good night!" Such proceedings rendered the Chartists liable to Government interference, and prosecutions were unhesitatingly undertaken. The great earnestness of the movement, however, was demonstrated by the nature of its errors, by the formation of a physical force party, and by the fact that the Chartist convention gravely considered the mad proposal for holding "a sacred month"—that is to say, a month in which the people should abstain from labour in order to force Parliament to yield to the demands made in the Charter. The movement excited compassion in the minds of many men, but its excesses strengthened the hands of the Government, who imprisoned many of its prominent members. The popular attachment to one of the imprisoned Chartists—

Henry Vincent—was so strong as to lead to a movement on Newport, where he was imprisoned, by a body of armed men with a view to his release, and to the incitement thereafter to a general rising. The march on Newport was well planned. Three divisions were to unite at Risca, and march to Newport under command to Frost, a Newport magistrate who had identified himself with the Chartist movement, and who had refused to resign his commission at the suggestion of Lord John Russell during the meetings of the Chartist convention. The plan of the attack was, however, not successfully carried out. The divisions failed to join at the rendezvous at the appointed hour, and Frost's own division, marching on alone, at an hour much later than originally intended, found the town authorities prepared for them, and were routed with a loss of 10 killed and 50 wounded. The leaders of all three divisions were arrested, tried, and sentenced to death, but had their sentences commuted to transportation. The development of these serious episodes in our history is traceable to the deaf ear turned by Parliament to the petitions of the people for a reconsideration of the subject of Reform. The chequered history of the Chartists could only be adequately traced in a volume specially devoted to this branch of the Reform movement. Suffice it to say, that ever and anon between the intervals of Government prosecution and dissensions in their own ranks, the Chartists were able to show to Parliament that no topic so readily united the people and awakened their enthusiasm as Parliamentary Reform, and that no treatment so exasperated them as the refusal of Parliament to recognise the justice of the demand for an extension of the representation of the people. To such refusal was due the revival and partial adoption of "the sacred month" scheme, and the renewal of riots. To such refusal was owing the fresh outbreak of Chartist sympathies in 1848, and the Kennington Common meeting, in view of which the Duke of Wellington made military preparations extensive enough to put down an armed insurrection. And though the failings and mistakes of the Chartist leader—Feargus O'Connor—and the discovery of an enormous number of fictitious signatures to the last monster Chartist petition, led to the ignominious extinction of the movement, the succeeding generation has paid no mean tribute to the principles which gave it strength. The third and fourth points of the Charter are the law of the land to-day; the fifth and the sixth are avowed articles in the political creed of at least one of our Cabinet Ministers. The franchise has been and is being lowered, not so far as indicated in the first point of the Charter, but to an extent which the Chartists would probably have been delighted to accept as a compromise. For annual parliaments there is at present no demand, but for the shortening of the duration of the parliament to some extent it will probably be found that public opinion will be ready as soon as more urgent questions are decided.

From this time forward Reform was a constantly recurring parliamentary question. Mr

Hume proposed a resolution in favour of household suffrage, triennial parliaments, electoral districts, and the ballot, and did the great service of eliciting from Lord John Russell a repudiation of the opinion which had given him the name of Finality Jack. Lord John denied the people household suffrage, but uttered those significant words in the mouth of a statesman :—"The time is at hand, if it has not already come, when some reform must be made in our representative system." The time was at hand, too, when Lord John Russell was to be compelled himself to propose the reform. Hume's motion for a Radical bill was refused year after year; but in 1851, Mr. Locke King's proposal to bring in a bill to assimilate the county to the borough franchise was carried against the Government, and was only defeated on a second reading because the Minister pledged himself to deal with the subject in the following session.

The Irish parliamentary franchise, it should be here noted, had in 1850 been reduced to £12 in the counties and £8 in the boroughs.

With the year 1852 commenced a series of abortive Government Reform Bills. To the last one before the Household Suffrage Act of 1867 the main interest attaches, and it will suffice to exhibit the others in the following list :—

1852. Lord John Russell's Bill—Proposals :— A £20 rating franchise for counties ; £5 rating franchise for boroughs ; a vote to be given to payers of income-tax or assessed taxes to the amount of 40s. a year; sixty-seven small borough constituencies to be increased by the addition of neighbouring places ; property qualification of members to be abolished ; omission from the oath of the words "on the true faith of a Christian " ; Ministers merely changing one office for another not to be required to vacate their seats.—Bill withdrawn on account of ministerial resignation.

1854. Lord John Russell's Bill—Proposals :— Votes to be given to £10 householders in counties if rated not lower than £5 ; to persons in boroughs rated at £6 ; to persons receiving a salary of £100 annually, otherwise than as weekly wages; to receivers of £10 per annum dividend from Funds, Bank stock, or East India Company's stock; to payers of direct taxes to the amount of 40s. Boroughs with fewer than 300 electors to be disfranchised, boroughs with fewer than 500 electors to be limited to one representative. Redistribution proposals included the creation of towns with 100,000 inhabitants into three-cornered constituencies, *i.e.*, boroughs with three members, electors having but two votes; and the enfranchisement of rising towns and London University.—Bill withdrawn on account of the Crimean war.

1859. Mr. Disraeli's Bill—Proposals :—To extend the county franchise to £10 householders; to maintain the existing franchise in boroughs, but give votes to fundholders and holders of Bank or East India stock yielding £10 per annum; to possessors of £60 in the savings bank, to recipients of £20 pensions from the naval, military, or civil services, to occupants of portions of houses rented at £20; to graduates, ministers of religion, members of the legal and medical professions, and certain schoolmasters ; fifteen small boroughs to be deprived of one member each to provide eight additional county members and members to large towns having no representative. Mr. Walpole and Mr. Henley retired from the Ministry on account of the proposed assimilation of county and borough franchise.—Bill rejected on second reading, an amendment by Lord John Russell condemning the county proposals and demanding an extended suffrage in the boroughs being adopted by 330 to 291.

1860. Lord John Russell's Bill.—Proposals :— £10 county franchise ; £6 borough rental franchise ; twenty-five towns to lose one member ; spare seats to be distributed in large counties, and to Chelsea, Kensington, Birkenhead, Stalybridge, Burnley, and London University, and as third seats to Liverpool, Manchester, Birmingham, and Leeds.—Bill abandoned, the opposition being strong, and Lord Palmerston not anxious to carry it.

No more Government Reform Bills were heard

of until 1866, but in the meantime, Mr. Locke
King and Mr. Baines kept the topic alive, and
it was impossible for any Ministry to allow the
question to remain much longer unsettled.
Mr. Locke King had the distinction of being the
first to accomplish one of the objects of the
People's Charter—the abolition of the property
qualification of members. Mr. King kept
bringing forward a bill to reduce the county
franchise to the level of that in the towns.
Mr. Baines persevered with his Borough Franchise Bill, proposing a £6 occupation franchise
in boroughs. The only measure of representation Parliament would pass, however, was one
assigning four seats which had for some time
been at the disposition of the House by reason
of the disfranchisement of Sudbury in 1844, and
of St. Albans in 1852, for bribery. Two seats
were given to the West Riding of Yorkshire, one
to South Lancashire, and one to Birkenhead.

Mr. Gladstone may be said to have made his
début as a Reformer in 1864, when he made in
Parliament, on the motion of Mr. Baines, a

speech which caused the working classes to look to him for their future enfranchisement. Capable citizenship was even then his view of the title to the franchise. " I venture to say," he said, " that every man who is not presumably incapacitated by some consideration of personal unfitness, or of political danger, is morally entitled to come within the pale of the constitution." It rested with the opponents of Reform, Mr. Gladstone said, to show the necessity for excluding some forty-nine fiftieths of the working classes from the vote. It was not difficult for him to show, what has been made clear in previous chapters of this work, that the working classes had been excluded from the franchise by the operation of the Act of 1832, and he remarked upon the curious anomaly, that while the social condition, the education, and the fitness generally of the working classes to exercise the duties of citizenship had advanced, their share in the suffrage had, by the gradual dying out of the ancient franchises, declined since the passing of the Act of 1832. The splendid behaviour of the Lancashire

operatives during the time of the cotton famine
had greatly impressed the mind of Mr. Gladstone,
and he was further predisposed in their favour
by the great success of the co-operative movement among working men in the north of
England. From this date, therefore, when Mr.
Gladstone, notwithstanding the anti-Reform
tendencies of his chief, Lord Palmerston, and
the fact that he was then holding the post of
Chancellor of the Exchequer, declared in favour
of Reform, the working classes felt that they
had a friend in the ranks of the Government.
They had already a very staunch friend outside
the Government. This was Mr. John Bright.

Mr. Bright had no hesitation about Reform,
or the shape it should take. He had no fear of
manhood suffrage, and was the idol of its advocates. But manhood suffrage was not the
scheme he preferred. He took up the original
position of Mr. Grey and the opinion of Mr.
Fox, and he argued for household suffrage as
the project of Reform which it was the most
reasonable to adopt. He advocated this mode

of Reform as the most reasonable that could be adopted. He was also a persistent advocate of the ballot, and had a bill prepared, though it never came before Parliament, for carrying into effect both those objects. Both measures he has had the happiness of seeing adopted, but the way in which his plan of household suffrage suddenly became the law of the land was to him and to all others an almost bewildering surprise.

Mr. Gladstone being leader of the House of Commons in the Ministry of Earl Russell (as Lord John Russell had now become) introduced a Reform Bill on the 12th March, 1866. It was preceded by a curious measure brought in by Mr. Clay, the member for Hull, who proposed to base the claim to the franchise on an educational qualification. Any man who passed an examination in reading, writing, spelling, and the four rules of arithmetic by the Civil Service Commissioners, was to receive a certificate entitling him to vote. It need hardly be said that this bill was withdrawn. Mr. Gladstone's Reform Bill was a moderate one, designed apparently to

conciliate opposition. Mr. Bright, though his
opinions were in favour of a measure more
advanced, afterwards characterised it as a measure of "a singular and most honest simplicity."
The county franchise proposed was a £14
occupation franchise, the occupation being an
occupation of house and land. The bill contemplated a £7 borough franchise. The compound householder in the boroughs was to be
put on the ratebook and so be entitled to the vote,
and tenants of portions of a house, or lodgers
paying £10 clear yearly value, were to be enfranchised. Mr. Gladstone's calculation was
that the bill would admit to the franchise
400,000 new voters. The Chancellor of the
Exchequer (that was then Mr. Gladstone's office)
excused the Government for not proposing a
lower franchise by the plea that it was not well
on general grounds of political prudence to
make changes of too sudden and extensive a
character in the depositaries of power. The
strongest opposition to the introduction of this
measure came from Mr. Lowe and Mr. Hors-

man, both on the Liberal side, whom Mr. Bright humorously described as forming a party of two, but a party comparable to a Scotch terrier, whose head could not be distinguished from the tail. The party, however, was destined to grow larger, and the name by which its adherents were distinguished was derived from another sally of Mr. Bright's humour. Mr. Horsman was described as the first of the new party, who had expressed his great grief, who had retired into his political Cave of Adullam, and who had called about him every one that was in distress, and every one that was discontented. Henceforward the Whig opponents of the bill were known as Adullamites, and there was an unexpected rush of members to the " Cave." Earl Grosvenor specially embarrassed the Government by bringing forward an amendment to the second reading, designed to force the Government to bring forward their whole Reform scheme— namely, their Scotch and Irish bills, and their plan of redistribution—before proceeding with the franchise bill. The debates were marked by much brilliant speaking, and by a great dread on the part both of Whigs and Tories of the enfranchisement of great numbers of the people, and Mr. Gladstone was strongly advised, notwithstanding a declaration made by him in the country, that he had crossed the Rubicon, burnt his boats, and broken down his bridges, to rebuild his boats and bridges and recross the river. From the adoption of the Government measure, Mr. Disraeli predicted successive extensions of the franchise, and a cessation of all command over the executive. He said, that though he was convinced that it was the opinion of the thoughtful portion of the community that the choicest members of the working classes should form a part, and no unimportant part, of the estate of the Commons, they recoiled from attaining that result by an undistinguishing reduction of the franchise. He wished to avert the calamities which must ensue from the establishment of our institutions upon American institutions. Mr. Gladstone, in his reply, ridiculed the notion that a proposal to add to the constituencies 200,000 of the lower middle classes, and about the same number of the working classes, was a reconstruction of the Constitution upon American principles ; but he only carried the second reading of his bill by five votes in a remarkably full House of 631 members. Such a small majority left no chance of carrying the measure, unless by concession to the Opposition. Mr. Gladstone had already agreed to show the Government intentions, by placing the other bills on the table after the second reading. He had now to agree to commit the franchise and redistribution * bills to one Committee, with

---

* The redistribution proposals were as follow :—1. To withdraw one member from every borough having a population under 8,000. 2. To group boroughs so as to give them one or two members according as their population was under or over 15,000. The groups were to be—

Woodstock, Abingdon, and Wallingford.
Liskeard, Bodmin, and Launceston.
Totnes, Ashburton, and Dartmouth.
Bridport, Honiton, and Lyme.
Wareham and Dorchester.
Harwich and Maldon.
Evesham, Tewkesbury, and Cirencester.
Leamington and Andover.
Leominster and Ludlow.

. a view to their amalgamation, and he had to
accept defeat on a motion by Sir R. Knightley,

> Eye and Thetford.
> Arundel, Horsham, Midhurst, and Petersfield.
> Calne, Chippenham, and Malmesbury.
> Wells and Westbury.
> Marlborough and Devizes.
> Thirsk, Ripon, and Knaresborough.
> Northallerton and Richmond.

3. Twenty-six seats were to be given to English counties.
A third member was allotted to Liverpool, Manchester,
Birmingham, and Leeds, as towns with a population of
over 200,000 ; and a second member to Salford.   Tower
Hamlets was to be divided into two sections, each returning two members.   Chelsea and Kensington were
to be united and to return two members ; and one member
was to be given to each unrepresented borough having a
population exceeding 18,000.   London University was to
have one member.   Seven seats were to be given to Scotland, so as to give an additional member to Ayr, Lanark,
and Aberdeen.   A third member was offered to Glasgow,
a third to Edinburgh, a second to Dundee, and one to the
Scotch Universities.   In Scotland the voting qualification was to be the same as in England, excepting as
regarded the property qualification, which, however, was
reduced to £5.   In Ireland it was proposed to join
Bandon with Kinsale, Portarlington with Athlone, and
Dungarvan with Enniskillen ; to provide a member for

instructing the Committee to combine with the bill provision for the better prevention of bribery and corruption. The Government successfully resisted a proposal by Lord Stanley to postpone the consideration of their franchise clauses until after their redistribution bill, and also defeated by 297 to 283 a motion by Mr. Walpole to substitute a £20 occupation franchise for a £14 franchise in counties, and another by Mr. Ward Hunt proposing to substitute rating for rental. A concession was exacted from Mr. Gladstone in regard to the county occupation, which he agreed need not comprise a house if some security were devised against the multiplication of joint tenancies. This concession greatly dissatisfied his own supporters.

At last after weary fighting the bill was finally upset by one of the " Cave " men, Lord Dunkellin, who on the 18th of June, proposed to substitute a £6 rating franchise for a £7 rental.

Dublin city, for Cork county, and for Queen's University. Other constituencies were to be enlarged by union with other places.

The argument adduced in favour of this alteration was that a rating clause would prevent a descent to universal suffrage. Its effect however was regarded as practically raising the borough franchise to £9, and aiming at the exclusion of working classes. The numbers, for the amendment 315, as against 304 in its favour, decided the fate of the Ministry. The bill was killed by the combination of Tory and Whig against it. Lord John Russell resigned, and Lord Derby was called to office.

What happened under the next administration has given a special interest to the speeches made by the new Ministers to their constituents. Mr. Disraeli intimated that the new Ministry would not, when they dealt with the subject of Reform, attempt to remodel the institutions of this country upon any foreign type whatever—American or French. He complained that it was impossible to understand whether the measure of the last Ministry was founded on the rights of man, or the rights of numbers. His views did not recognise that the rights of man should prevail in our legislature, or that a numerical majority should dictate to an ancient nation of various political orders and classes. What his Government wished to see was that the electoral power should be deposited with the best men of all classes, and that was the principle on which, if called upon, they would propose to legislate. Lord Stanley described Mr. Gladstone's measure as having gone further, as regarded the franchise, than the majority of the House of Commons was prepared to follow. In Parliament, Lord Derby professed a willingness to see a large increase in the number of electors, but feared that the portion of the community who were most clamorous for a Reform Bill, were not those who would be satisfied with any measure that was likely to be concurred in by the two great political parties. There was certainly nothing reassuring to the Reformers in these declarations.

Now arose a great public agitation, recalling, in regard to the numbers that took part in it, the great demonstrations in 1831--2. The answer of the populace to the ministerial declarations was a flat demand for "residential and registered manhood suffrage and the ballot." Much dissatisfaction was felt at the course taken by Earl Russell's Cabinet in resigning instead of appealing to the country, but a great crowd, which at Trafalgar Square had censured the late Ministers for this action, indicated their belief in Mr. Gladstone's friendship for Reform by proceeding to his house and cheering him lustily. The excitement of the Reformers was increased by the attempt of the police, under instructions from the Government, to prevent the Reform League using Hyde Park for the purpose of political demonstrations. A great procession, Mr. Beales at its head, was nevertheless organised, and the demand for admission to the park was made. The promoters of the demonstration, in accordance with a previously arranged plan, led the procession away towards Trafalgar Square, but the enormous crowd which had gathered at the park threw down the railings, both in Bayswater Road, and in Park Lane.

Nearly every great town had its monster Reform demonstration in this recess, and at all these great meetings the cry from the working classes was for manhood suffrage and the ballot. Mr. Lowe, who had animadverted strongly on the vices of the working classes, was the object of special odium, while Mr. Bright was fêted in every town to which he cared to accept an invitation.

In this state of affairs, the Government could not afford to let Reform alone, but much amusement was created in Parliament when Mr. Disraeli announced that this question, on which their predecessors had been turned out, ought no longer to be a question which should determine the fate of Cabinets. He insisted on first proceeding by way of resolutions, and these resolutions, while in favour of an increased electorate, and more direct representation to the labouring class, declared it contrary to the Constitution to give any one class or interest a predominating power over the rest of the community. The resolutions further pointed to a settlement of

the franchise on the principle of rating, to dual
voting, the use of voting papers, and the
enlargement - of borough boundaries. The
opinion of Parliament being strongly urged in
favour of procedure by bill, a measure was
promised, but the Houses and the country were
soon greatly surprised to learn that the attempt
of the Conservative Government to formulate
their proposals in legislative shape had resulted
in the secession from the Cabinet of three of its
prominent members, the Earl of Carnavon, Colonial Secretary, Viscount Cranbourne (the present Marquis of Salisbury), Indian Secretary, and
General Peel, Secretary for War. The majority
of the Government had in fact determined on
household suffrage in boroughs, hoping to guard
against its effects by the provisions for plurality
of voting. The three members of the Cabinet
who had retired had no faith in the safeguards
or compensations. Their want of faith was
amply justified by the result. Not one of the
safeguards was retained. To every important
attack the Ministry yielded, and what was called

the Conservative surrender on the question of Reform was complete, while those who, like Mr. Lowe, had helped to throw out the late Government were astounded at the acts of those whom they had admitted to power. The changes made in the bill were described by Mr. Gladstone as necessary on the second reading, but no one ever dreamt that every demand thus formulated by the leader of an Opposition would be complied with. The original provisions of the bill and its provisions as it received the Royal assent are shown below :—

ORIGINAL BILL.	BILL AS PASSED.
Household franchise in boroughs, conditional on *two* years' residence and personal payment of rates.	Household franchise, conditional as *one* year's residence, compound householder abolished, the occupier alone being rated.
£15 franchise in counties.	£12 franchise in counties.
Educational franchise for graduates or associates in arts of any university of the United Kingdom, for those who passed senior middle	*No* educational franchise.

ORIGINAL BILL.	BILL AS PASSED.
class examinations, for clergymen, professional men, and schoolmasters.	
A pecuniary franchise for savings bank depositors with balance of £50, fund-holders of like amount, and direct tax-payers to the amount of £1 per annum.	*No* pecuniary franchise.
Dual voting—a provision entitling the holder of the pecuniary franchise to vote for the same borough, in respect of any franchise involving occupation of premises and payment of rates.	*No* dual voting.
Voting papers.	*No* voting papers.
No lodger franchise.	A £10 lodger franchise.
No cumulative vote or three-cornered constituencies, these being declared by Mr. Disraeli as erroneous in principle and pernicious in practice.	*Four* three-cornered constituencies.
Twenty-three towns under 7,000 in population to be deprived of one member, and Totness, Reigate, Great Yarmouth,	Thirty-five towns below 10,000 in population deprived of one member. Eleven boroughs ultimately disfranchised.

ORIGINAL BILL.	BILL AS PASSED.
and Lancaster, convicted of corrupt practices, to be disfranchised.	
Fourteen of the new seats to be given to boroughs, 15 to counties, and one to London University.	Eighteen of the new seats to boroughs, 25 to counties, and 1 to London University, 1 seat being afterwards given to Wales, and 7 to Scotland.
No third members to Manchester, Liverpool, Birmingham, and Leeds.	Third members given to Manchester, Liverpool, Birmingham, and Leeds.

Among these alterations those creating the three-cornered constituencies are due to the House of Lords. In the House of Commons the fiercest battle raged over the compound householder, and by the aid of a defection in the Liberal ranks of a number of gentlemen who became known as the Tea Room party Mr. Gladstone's opposition to the bill was for a time hampered. The acceptance by Mr. Disraeli later in the session of Mr. Hodgkinson's amendment abolishing the compound householder greatly astounded everybody. The fancy franchises, as Mr. Bright and Mr. Lowe called them, were abandoned in the face of the firm opposition offered them. The change of the period of residence from two years to one was effected on a motion by Mr. Ayrton. A crisis was supposed to have occurred at this stage, as Mr. Disraeli refused to proceed with the bill, until he had consulted his colleagues, but the next night the decision of the House was accepted, and the bill went rapidly forward, Liberals joining heartily in the work of amending the measure to suit their views. Mr. Disraeli conceded to a Liverpool member, Mr. Horsfall, what he had refused to Mr. Laing and Mr. Gladstone—a third member to Manchester, Liverpool, and Birmingham; he voluntarily added Leeds. It was this last concession that provoked from General Peel the caustic remark that he should now conclude that there was "nothing with less vitality than a vital point, nothing so insecure as the securities that the bill offered, and nothing so elastic as the conscience of a Cabinet Minister." The feelings with which Tories like Lord Cranbourne regarded this remarkable work of a Conservative Government was indicated in his bitter speech on the third reading, in which he complained of a policy of legerdemain and a political betrayal which had no parallel in our parliamentary annals, and struck at the root of that mutual confidence which was the soul of our party government, and on which only the strength and freedom of our representative institutions could be sustained. In the House of Lords the Earl of Derby confessed that he had taken "a leap in the dark," and Earl Granville told how in the town the story was current that the Ministry had "dished the Whigs." But the country had gained a Household Suffrage Act.

In Scotland, by an Act passed in 1868, the franchise in boroughs was fixed on the same terms as in England, and in counties the occupation tenure was fixed at £14 or upwards as appearing on the valuation rolls of the county. It was by the total disfranchisement of certain English boroughs that the seven new members were given to Scotland.

By the Irish Act passed in the same year, no new seats were given to Ireland and the franchise was reduced to £4 only in boroughs.

RESULTS OF REFORM ACTS OF 1867-8.

Eleven English Boroughs disfranchised.—Arundel, Ashburton, Dartmouth, Honiton, Lancaster, Lyme Regis, Reigate, Thetford, Totness, Yarmouth, and Wells.

Thirty-five English Boroughs deprived of one Member.—Evesham, Marlborough, Harwich, Richmond, Lymington, Chippenham, Bridport, Stamford, Wycombe, Poole, Knaresborough, Andover, Leominster, Tewkesbury, Ludlow, Ripon, Huntingdon, Maldon, Buckingham, Newport, Malton, Tavistock, Lewes, Cirencester, Bodmin, Great Marlow, Devizes, Hertford, Dorchester, Lichfield, Cockermouth, Bridgnorth, Guildford, Chichester, and Windsor.

One new Borough with two Members.—Chelsea, including Fulham, Hammersmith, and Kensington.

One old Borough divided, each division to be a new Borough with two Members.—Tower Hamlets, divided into Tower Hamlets and Hackney.

Nine new Boroughs with one Member.—Darlington, The Hartlepools, Stockton, Barnsley, Staleybridge, Wednesbury, Middlesborough, Dewsbury, and Gravesend.

Thirteen new Divisions of Counties returning two Members.—Mid Cheshire, East Derbyshire, East Devonshire, North East Essex, Mid Kent, North East Lancashire, South East Lancashire, Mid Lincolnshire, South East Norfolk, Mid Somerset, East Stafford, Mid Surrey, and South West Riding.

Two Scotch Boroughs gaining an extra Member.—Glasgow (a third), Dundee (a second).

Scotch Counties united losing one Member.—Selkirk and Peebles.

New Scotch Borough District.—The Border Burghs.

Three Scotch Counties gaining extra Members.—Lanark, Ayr, and Aberdeen.

Enfranchised Universities.—London, Edinburgh with St. Andrews, Glasgow with Aberdeen.

CHAPTER X.

MR. GLADSTONE'S REFORM BILL.

THE passing of the Household Suffrage Bills of 1867–8 was followed, after the lapse of a few years, by the realisation of one more point of the Charter. The Ballot Bill, after being rejected by the Lords in 1871, was passed in 1872, with a clause requiring its renewal after a trial of eight years. This measure has not yet been made perpetual, but its renewal from year to year has not been seriously resisted.

The passing of a drastic Corrupt Practices Act contributes one most essential Reform—the guarding of the vote for a member of Parliament from undue influence. At the present moment two Reforms are called for—the assimilation of the county and borough franchise, and the redistribution of seats. The anomalies appealed to by those who demand these reforms are very striking and have naturally been made more prominent by the lowering of the borough franchise. It has been pointed out * that 151 towns and places, having over ten thousand inhabitants are virtually disfranchised, while Portarlington with 147 registered voters and not more than 2,000 inhabitants, can send a representative to St. Stephens; that the twenty-three smallest boroughs return forty-five members with 28,000 votes, a number which in Edinburgh can return but two members, while it takes three quarters of a million votes in nineteen constituencies to return a similar number of members: and that 33,000 electors in the counties return nineteen members, while Middlesex with the same number of electors returns only two. Ample materials for comparisons of this kind have lately been furnished in a parliamentary return moved for by Mr. Arthur Arnold, giving complete electoral

* In "The Assimilation of the Borough and County Franchises," a lecture delivered to the Haslemere Liberal Association, by Edmund Routledge.

statistics for the counties and boroughs of the
United Kingdom. It appears from these
statistics that the following is the present state
of the electorate :—

	England and Wales.	Scotland.	Ireland.	Total.
Borough voters ...	1,651,732	210,789	58,021	1,920,542
County voters ...	966,721	99,652	165,997	1,232,370
Total	2,618,453	310,441	224,018	3,152,912

Four boroughs—Beverley, Bridgewater, Sligo,
and Cashel—have been disfranchised since the
last Reform Act, and the total number of
members is now 651, though at the present
moment the membership is temporarily reduced
by the suspension of the writ in the case of a
number of boroughs in which corrupt practices
prevailed at the last election. Deducting from
651 eight university members, the remaining
643 are distributed thus :—

484 to England and Wales, representing an

area of 58,260 square miles, a population of 25,974,439, and 4,831,519 inhabited houses.

58 to Scotland, representing an area of 29,820 square miles, a population of 3,728,124, and 739,005 inhabited houses.

101 to Ireland, representing an area of 32,541 square miles, a population of 5,174,836, and 914,108 inhabited houses.

Upon the above figures calculations are already being made with reference to the coming redistribution of seats ; but it may be remarked that these are not exactly the bases upon which such calculations have previously been made. Lord Castlereagh calculated the number of members to which he thought Ireland entitled, upon a comparison into which there entered the relative population, imports, exports and revenue of the two countries. Having calculated the proportion of members to which Ireland would be entitled upon each basis separately, he added the totals, and, dividing the amount by the number of his bases, arrived at his average. It was afterwards pointed out that there had been errors in his calculations to the disadvantage of Ireland, and in 1832 the Irish members maintained that upon Lord Castlereagh's data they would be entitled to 178 members. The Irish members in 1832 also protested against any comparison with Scotland and England separately, maintaining that in any redistribution their claims should be considered, as they were at the Union, in relation to the total number of members for Great Britain.

The need for assimiliation of the county and borough franchise and redistribution has been admitted by Liberals at all events in the discussion of motions periodically raised by Mr. Trevelyan ; and the government of which he is now a member, came into power pledged to deal with these questions. To this task the Government has now set its hand.

The Representation of the People Bill, explained by Mr. Gladstone on the 28th of February, proposes to add to the number of electors in the United Kingdom nearly two million voters—the largest admission to the franchise ever made in this kingdom. " The enfranchisement of capable citizens," Mr. Gladstone has said, " be they few or be they many—and if they be many so much the better—is an addition to the strength of the state." * A novelty in Mr. Gladstone's proposals is the service franchise, by which he proposes to include in the extended household franchise all those responsible householders who are neither owners nor tenants, but who hold their houses as one of the conditions of their service. " The service franchise," Mr. Gladstone says, " is a far-reaching one : it goes to men of high class, who inhabit valuable houses as the officers of great institutions, and it descends to the humble classes, who are the servants of the gentry, the servants of the farmer, or the servants of some other employers of labour, who are neither owners nor tenants, and who in many cases cannot be held as tenants in consequence of the essential condition intended to be realised through their labour, and who fully fulfil the posi-

* See extracts from Mr. Gladstone's speeches in Appendix.

tion of responsible inhabitant householders." Mr.
Gladstone has stated his other proposals thus :—
"In the future borough franchise, if our proposals be adopted, there will be a fourfold occupation or householding franchise, namely, there
will be the old clear yearly value franchise of the
Act of 1832,* there will be the lodger franchise
of the Act of 1867, there will be the service
franchise of the Act, as I trust, of 1884, and there
will be, what will be the most important of all,
the household franchise proposed in 1867, and
developed from its original narrow and stunted
proportions, partly by the votes of this House
and partly by subsequent Acts of Parliaments,
into what it is—namely, the principal franchise
of the cities and towns of the country. . . . With
the county franchise we propose to proceed as

* Of this franchise, Mr. Gladstone said :—"For reasons
which are partly of principle and partly with a view
to unity, we extend the £10 clear yearly value franchise
to cases where the occupation is of land without houses or
buildings. At present it may be for houses or buildings
alone, or houses or buildings with land. We extend it
to land alone without buildings."

follows—we propose to abolish the £50 franchise which I shall call for convenience sake the £50 rental franchise. We propose to abolish it, because two categories of franchise where only one is necessary are highly inconvenient in the rate-books and registration, and because we believe it is hardly possible that there will be any men entitled to this £50 rental franchise who will not come within the county franchise as we propose it in this bill. We propose to reduce the figure of the rated franchise of 1867 from £12 rateable value to £10 clear annual value. The household, the lodger, and the service franchise we propose to import into the counties precisely as they are now. We maintain the property franchise in principle, but we propose provisions which are brought forward in order to secure it against the abuses which are known in many parts of the country, and which, in some portions of the country, are grievous and menacing. The purpose of this bill, and I may say that the fundamental part of the structure of this bill, is in the direction and with the intention of bringing about a union of the three kingdoms in one nation, and essentially, so far as we can without undue complexity achieve it, not only in one measure, but in one and the same measure."

Genuine property franchises are thus left untouched by Mr. Gladstone's bill, but precautions are taken against the manufacture of fictitious qualifications hitherto known as faggot votes. Warned by the experience of 1866, Mr. Gladstone has declined, with the sanction of all his supporters, to burden his bill with redistribution clauses.* The question of rearrangement of seats is left for the subsequent consideration of Parliament. In the meantime, that question has, however, attracted more attention from opponents than even the provisions of the Franchise Bill itself, which indeed has not yet encountered direct opposition. The questions of the enfranchisement of women and proportional representation promise to take an important place in the

* See Mr. Gladstone's remarks on Redistribution and on the Irish Representation in Appendix.

new discussions of Reform. The advocates of proportional representation have to struggle against a difficulty in convincing people that any satisfactory plan has been, or can be, devised for securing that the Parliament shall be an absolutely true mirror of the various currents of opinion in the country, or that if such a plan could be produced, it would be desirable to adopt it in days when minorities have no difficulty in getting a fair hearing for their views out of Parliament, among the electors, and when they are somewhat apt to prove obstructive when in. Sooner or later the conclusion is likely to be arrived at, that the best guarantee for securing an adequate representation of popular opinion in Parliament, and yet giving a fair chance to minorities, is to be found in the maintenance of the old-fashioned system of election, combined with a reversion to the constitutional plan of frequent Parliaments. With shorter Parliaments the need of minority representation would cease to be felt. Controversy on the Irish representation is threatened, owing to the resolve of the Cabinet to mete out

to that country a full measure of justice, with perhaps some compensation for past ungenerous
treatment ; but the sketch of the History of
Reform attempted in these pages does not reveal
any ground of encouragement for those who in-
cline to snatch away a once-proffered concession
in the direction of an amended representation of
the people.   Neither does it, nor could any historical narrative of wider scope, afford reason for
gloom at the prospect of a Reform freely granted.
Whatever may have in the future to be written
of the Reform Bill of 1884, its initial successes
have never been excelled by any of its predecessors ; and no measure could show better
promise than one which has carried with it
through its second reading the sanction of a
united Liberal party, and which must bear
throughout its progress the prestige conferred
upon it by the magnificent majority of 130.

APPENDIX.

Extracts from the Speech of Mr. Gladstone in introducing the Representation of the People Bill, 1884.

THE "CAPABLE CITIZEN."

I am not prepared to discuss an admission to the franchise as it was discussed fifty years ago, when Lord Russell had to state with almost bated breath that he expected to add in the three kingdoms half a million to the constituencies. It is not now a question of nicely calculated less or more. I take my stand on the broad principle that the enfranchisement of capable citizens, be they few or be they many—and if they be many so much the better—gives an addition of strength to the State. The strength of the modern State lies in the representative system. I rejoice to think that in this happy country and under this happy Constitution we have other sources of strength in the respect paid to various orders of the State, and in the authority they enjoy, and in the unbroken course which has been allowed to most of our national traditions ; but still in the main it is the representative system which is the strength of the modern State in general, and of the State in this country in particular. Sir, I may say—it is an illustration which won't occupy more than a moment—that never has this great truth been so vividly illustrated as in the war of the American Republic. The convulsion of that country between 1861 and 1865 was perhaps the most frightful which ever assailed a national existence. The efforts which were made on both sides were marked. The exertions by which alone the movement was put down were not only extraordinary; they were what would antecedently have been called impossible, and they were only rendered possible by the fact that they proceeded from a nation where every capable citizen was enfranchised and had a direct and an energetic interest in the well-being and the unity of the State. Sir, the only question that remains in the general argument is, who are the capable citizens?—and, fortunately, that is a question which, on the present occasion, need not be argued at length, for it has been already settled—in the first place by a solemn legislative judgment acquiesced in by both parties in the State, and in the second place by the experience of the last more than fifteen years. Who, Sir, are the capable citizens of the State? Whom it is proposed to enfranchise? It is proposed in the main to enfranchise the county population on the footing, and according to the measure, that has already been administered to the population of the towns. What are the main constituents of the county population? First of all, they are the minor tradesmen of the country, and the skilled labourers and artisans in all the common arts of life, and especially in connection with our great mining industry. Is there any doubt that these are capable citizens? You (the Opposition) have yourselves asserted it by enfranchising them in the towns, and we can only say that we heartily subscribe to the assertion. But besides the artisans and the small tradesmen scattered throughout our rural towns we have also to deal with the peasantry of this country. Is there any doubt that the peasantry of the country are capable citizens, qualified for enfranchisement, qualified to make good use of their power as voters? Again, this is a question which has been solved for us by the first and second Reform Bills, because many of the constituencies which under the name of towns are now represented in this House are really rural communities, based upon a peasant constituency, and for my part I should be quite ready to fight the battle of the peasant upon general and argumentative grounds. I believe the peasant generally to be, not in the highest sense, but in a very real sense a skilled labourer. He is not a man tied down to one mechanical exercise of his physical powers. He is a man who must do many things requiring the exercise of active intelligence. But as I say, it is not necessary to argue on that ground, first of all because we have got his friends here — (Ministerial laughter, as Mr. Gladstone indicated the Opposition)—from whom we must anticipate great zeal for his enfranchisement ; and secondly, because the question has been settled by legislative authority in the towns, and by a long practical experience. If he has a defect it is that he is too ready, perhaps, to work with and to accept the influence of his superiors—superiors, I mean, in worldly station. But that is the last defect that you (the Opposition) will be disposed to plead against him, and it is a defect that we do not feel ourselves entitled to plead, and that we are not at all inclined to plead. We are ready to take him as he is, and joyfully bring him within the reach of this last and highest privilege of the Constitution. There is only one other word, Sir, to add on this part of the subject. The present position of the franchise is one of greater and grosser anomaly than any in which it has been heretofore placed, because the exclusion of persons of the same class and the same description is more palpable and more pervading than before, being, in fact, spread over the whole country, and persons being excluded in one place while the same persons have been admitted in another. I wish just to call the attention of the House to an important fact connected with this part of the question, and it is the frequent occurrence of that which the House detests, and which we in this Bill shall endeavour to avoid—namely, the infliction of personal disfranchisement. Observe how the present state of the franchise law brings this about. It is known and well understood that a labourer must follow his labour. Where his labour goes, where the works go in which he is employed, he must follow. He cannot remain at a great distance from them ; and the instance I will give— and though I am not personally conversant with it I believe there is no doubt about the fact—is an instance publicly mentioned to me, and I think singularly applicable. It is that of the ship-building works on the Clyde. Those works were within the precincts of the city of Glasgow, and the persons who laboured in them were able to remain within the city, being near their work, and at the same time to enjoy the franchise. But the marvellous enterprise of Glasgow, which has made that city the centre and crown of the ship-building business of the world, could not be confined within the limits of the city of Glasgow, and by compulsion of necessity moved down the river. As the trade moved down the river the artisans required to move down the river with it. That was a matter of necessity, and the obedience to that necessity under the present franchise involves wholesale dis-franchisement. That is an argument which is sufficient for disposing of the general question. The whole popu-lation, I rejoice to think, have liberty of speech, they have liberty of writing, they have liberty of meeting in public, they have liberty of private association, they have liberty of petitioning Parliament. And these privileges are not privileges taken away from us, diminishing our power and security. They are all of them privileges on the existence of which our security depends. Without them we could not be secure. I ask you to confer upon the very same classes the crowning privilege of voting for a representative in Parliament, and then I say we who are strong now as a nation and a State shall by virtue of that change be stronger still.

REDISTRIBUTION.

WE are determined, as far as depends upon us, not to deck-load our Franchise Bill. (Cheers.) We consider that we have filled the hold with a good and sufficient cargo, but the deck-loading of it would be a preliminary to its foundering ; and were we with that impression—nay, not merely impression, but with that conviction and knowledge—to encumber our Bill with unnecessary weight, we should be traitors to the cause which we profess to have taken in hand, and we therefore will have nothing to do with giving encouragement to such a policy. . . . A fortiori, in our opinion it would be absurd for us to attempt to deal in the same measure with what is termed redistribution . . . I admit that legislation on redistribution ought to follow legislation on the franchise at an early date—at the earliest date—and the earliest date will be next session ; and it is for that reason that we have brought forward the Franchise Bill of 1884, in order that within the natural life of the present Parliament there may be plenty of time to deal with the question . . . I have not the least objection to make a little sketch of my own views upon redistribution. I think when a measure of redistribution comes, it must be a large measure of redistribution. I do not know whether it need be so large as the measure of 1831 ; but at any rate it must be nearer the measure of 1831 than the one of 1867. At the same time I am not personally at all favourable to what is called the system of electoral districts, or to the adoption of any pure population scale. I cannot pretend to have the fear and horror which some people have with regard to the consequences of electoral districts in many places. My objection is a very simple and practical one. It will be two-fold—in the first place, electoral districts would involve a great deal of unnecessary displacement and disturbance of traditions. But my second objection is—and that I regard as a very important one—that I don't believe that public opinion at all requires it, and I doubt whether it would warrant it. Next I should say that in a sound measure of redistribution the distinction between town and country, known to electoral law as borough and shire, ought to be maintained. Although our franchise is nearly identical, that is not the question. The question is whether there is not in the pursuits and associations of the place, and in its social circumstances, a difference between town and country, between borough and shire, which it is expedient, becoming, and useful to maintain. Next I would say that I would respect within moderate limits the individuality of constituencies, and not attempt to place towns which have had representation for many generations precisely and mathematically upon the footing of towns that have not. I am certainly disposed to admit that very large and highly-concentrated populations need not have and perhaps ought not to have quite so high a proportional share in the representation of the country as rural and dispersed populations, because the actual political power in these concentrated masses is

sharper, quicker, and more vehement. That consideration, of course, would apply most of all to the metropolis.
Another consideration I would lay down is this—I would
not reduce the proportional share of representation
accorded to Ireland. In my opinion some regard ought
to be had to relative nearness and distance. Take Scotland, for example ; the nearest part of it is 350 miles off
and some parts of it are 700 miles off. It is impossible
to say that numerical representation meets the case,
though I grant it is pretty well made up for by the shrewd-
ness of the men whom Scotland sends ; but it is her virtue
and good fortune which cause her to make so excellent a
choice. Undoubtedly representation is exercised under
greater difficulties, and it is fair that those parts of the
country which like Scotland are separated by great dis-
tances, not omitting the element of sea, should be more
liberally dealt with in proportion to the representatives
they ought to send. There is one other proposition which
I am disposed to lay with considerable hesitation and not
as giving a final opinion. Speaking roughly what will
happen will be this. Smaller boroughs, so many of which
are in the south of England, must yield seats for London
and other great towns, for the counties, and, thirdly for
Scotland and the north of England. Scotland and the
North of England have perhaps the largest and most
salient of all these claims. That operation certainly leads
to a proposition, if under the altered circumstances of
Parliament and its increasing business Parliament were
disposed to entertain it, but which it has not yet favourably
entertained, and I think ought not to entertain, for a
limited addition to the number of its members. I ask no
assent of the House to that proposition. All I say is, I
do not exclude it from the view of the whole circumstances of the case ; and it may be found materially to

Q

facilitate the operation, which is not one altogether of slight magnitude or difficulty. Finally, when redistribution has come forward, then come all the propositions with regard to minority representation and with regard to modes of voting. These very important subjects will have to be fully considered, but I myself see no cause to change the opinion I have always entertained with regard to them. I admit they have claims which ought to receive the full and impartial consideration of Parliament.

ESTIMATED RESULTS OF THE BILL.

In 1832 there was passed what was considered a Magna Charta of British liberties ; but that Magna Charta of British liberties added, according to the previous estimate of Lord John Russell, half a million, while according to the results considerably less than half a million were added to the entire constituency of the three countries. After 1832 we come to 1866. At that time the total constituency of the United Kingdom reached 1,364,000. By the Bills which were passed between 1867 and 1869 that number was raised to 2,448,000. And now, Sir, under the action of the present law the constituency has reached in round numbers what I would call 3,000,000. I will not enter into details ; but what is the increase we are going to make? There is a basis of computation, but it is a basis which affords, I admit, ground for conjecture and opinion. The basis of computation is the present ratio in towns between houses and the number of town electors. Of course we have availed ourselves of that basis for the purpose of computation. I have gone into the matter as carefully as I can, and the best results I can attain are these. The Bill, if it passes as presented, will add to the English constituency over 1,300,000 persons. It will add to the Scotch constituency, Scotland being at present rather better provided than either of the other countries, over 200,000, and to the Irish constituency over 400,000. Or in the main to the present aggregate constituency of the United Kingdom taken at 3,000,000, it will add 2,000,000 more, nearly as much as was added since 1867, and more than four times as much as in 1832. Surely, I say, that is worth not endangering. Surely that is worth some sacrifice. This is a measure with results such as I have ventured to sketch them that ought to bring home to the mind of every man favourable to the extension the solemn question what course he is to pursue in regard to it. I hope the House will look at it as the Liberal party in 1831 looked at the Reform Bill of that date, and determined that they would waive criticism of minute details, that they would waive particular preferences and predilections, and would look at the broad scope and general effect of the measure. Do that upon this occasion. It is a Bill worth having, and if it is worth having again, it is a Bill worth your not endangering. Let us enter into no byeways which would lead us off the path marked out straight before us ; let us not wander on the hill-tops of speculation ; let us not wander among the fogs of doubt, but with a burning faith that enfranchisement is a good, that the people may be trusted, that the voters under the Constitution are the strength of the Constitution. What we want in order to carry this Bill, considering as I fully believe that the very large majority of this House are favourable to its principle—what we want in order to carry it is union and union only. What will endanger it is disunion and disunion only. Let us hold firmly together and success will crown our effort. You will as much as any former Parliament that has conferred great legislative benefits on the nation have your reward, and read your history in a nation's eyes, for you will have deserved it by the benefits you have conferred. You will have made this strong nation stronger still, stronger in union without ; stronger against its foes, if and when it has any ; stronger within in union between class and class, and in rallying all classes and portions of the community in one solid, compacted mass around the ancient throne which it has loved so well, and round the Constitution now to be more than ever free and more than ever powerful.

MR. GLADSTONE'S VIEWS ON IRISH REPRESENTATION.

(From his Speech on the Second Reading of the Representation of the People Bill, 7th April, 1884.)

"With regard to my own outline of redistribution, I am glad to see that so far as I know nearly the whole of the propositions that I laid down have been received in a favourable manner. The adverse criticism has been concentrated on a single opinion which I expressed—that, so far as I was able to judge, it would not be wise to reduce the number of Irish representatives, which stands at 103.

*　　*　　*　　*　　*　　*

I fully admit that at the present moment Ireland has but one-seventh of the population, and that, on the basis of one-seventh of the population, instead of 103 members Ireland is entitled only to 93 members. That is not a very great breadth of margin. But, in the first place, in my own mind I am not willing to assume that this continual decline of Irish population is a permanent or a normal factor. It may be that there are cases where a great reduction of population is a necessary road to a people's well-being. It may be that Ireland has pre-sented one of these cases. But it is a most painful thing, and that depletion is in itself a subject for regretful recollection, while the consequences produced by the dissemination of a population over the globe who carry away with them the idea that they have been driven from their homes are consequences painful enough for us all to bear in mind. I do not abandon the hope that Ireland may recover something of the ground she has lost. Con-sidering that it has been but once in fifty years that a question like this has been entertained I would certainly not assume the permanence of this continual descent in the numbers of the people of Ireland. And further, sir, I would say this—those who have been niggardly in former times, those who have been unjust in former times, must be very cautious when they come to plead on their own behalf for the strictest application of laws of which they might have claimed the strictest application if they had never deviated from them themselves.

It is not a very large question, take it which way you will. But look back to 1832, and see how we dealt with Ireland on that occasion. Ireland had then almost three-tenths of the population of the United Kingdom, and we gave her considerably less than one-sixth of the represen-tation. I don't think we should say now that that was handsome treatment ; and I could not entirely dismiss from my recollection that fact in coming to consider the Irish question, when we deal with the redistribution of seats in prosecution of the plan contemplated by the present Government. I do not wish to commit anyone. But I say it is not a desirable position for a great country to occupy—that it should claim the most rigid application of numerical laws when they tell in her favour, and to apply a very lax rule indeed when they tell against her. If Ireland in 1832, had been treated according to her numbers, the number of her members would be such that I am almost afraid to present it to the imagination of honourable gentlemen opposite. They would have been nearer 200 than 100. However, having stated what appears to me right on this subject, I must claim for myself that the view of the proposition that I threw out should be taken, as my noble friend near me (Lord Hartington) most justly said, in conjunction with the other propositions which I was inclined to submit for the favourable consideration of the House.

THE REPRESENTATION OF THE PEOPLE BILL, 1884.

[THE FOLLOWING IS THE TEXT OF MR. GLADSTONE'S BILL, WHICH WAS READ A FIRST TIME ON 3RD MARCH.]

A.D. 1884. *A Bill to Amend the Law relating to the Representation of the People of the United Kingdom.*

BE it enacted by the Queen's most Excellent Majesty, by and with the advice and consent of the Lords Spiritual and Temporal, and Commons, in this present Parliament assembled, and by the authority of the same, as follows :

Preliminary.

Short Title of Act.
1. This Act may be cited as the Representation of the People Act, 1884.

Extension of the Household and Lodger Franchise.

Uniform household and lodger franchise.
2. A uniform household and lodger franchise at elections shall be established in all counties and

boroughs throughout the United Kingdom, and *after the passing of this Act* every man possessed• of a household qualification or a lodger qualification shall, if the qualifying premises ·be situate in a county in England or Scotland, be entitled to be registered as a voter, and when registered to vote at an election for such county, and if the qualifying premises be situate in a county or borough in Ireland, be entitled to be registered as a voter, and to vote at an election for such county or borough.

3. Where a man himself inhabits any dwelling-house by virtue of any office, service, or employment, and the dwelling-house is not inhabited by any person under whom such man serves in such office, service, or employment, he shall be deemed for the purposes of this Act and of the Representation of the People Acts to be an inhabitant occupier of such dwelling-house as a tenant.

Tenure of house by office or service not to invalidate vote.

Prohibition of Multiplication of Votes.

4. Subject to the saving in this Act for existing voters, the following provisions shall after the passing of this Act have effect with reference to elections :

Restriction on faggot votes.

    (1.) A man shall not be entitled to be registered as a voter in respect of the ownership of any rentcharge except the owner of the whole of the tithe rentcharge of a rectory or vicarage.

    (2.) Where two or more men are owners either as joint tenants or as tenants in common of an estate in any land or tenement, one of such men, but not more than one, shall if his interest is sufficient to confer on him a qualification as a voter in respect of the ownership of such estate, be entitled (in the like cases and subject to the like conditions as if he were the sole owner) to be registered as a voter, and when registered to vote at an election.

Provided that where such owners have derived their interest by descent, succession, marriage, marriage settlement, or will, or where they occupy the land or tenement, and are bonâ fide engaged as partners carrying on trade or business thereon, each of such owners whose interest is sufficient to confer on him a qualification as a voter shall be entitled (in the like cases and subject to the like conditions as if he were sole owner) to be registered as a voter in respect of such ownership, and when registered to vote at an election, and the value of the interest of each such owner where not otherwise legally defined shall be ascertained by the division of the total value of the land or tenement equally among the whole of such owners.

Assimilation of Occupation Qualification.

Assimilation of occupation qualification.

5. Every man occupying any land or tenement in a county or borough in the United Kingdom of a clear yearly value of not less than ten pounds, shall be entitled, *after the passing of this Act*, to be registered as a voter, and when registered to vote at an election for such county or borough in respect of such occupation, subject to the like conditions

respectively as a man is, at the passing of this Act, entitled to be registered as a voter and to vote at an election for such county in respect of the county occupation franchise, and at an election for such borough in respect of the borough occupation franchise.

Supplemental Provisions.

6. A man shall not by virtue of this Act be entitled to be registered as a voter or to vote at any election for a county in respect of the occupation of any dwelling-house, lodgings, land, or tenement, situate in a borough. *(Voter not to vote for county in respect of occupation of property in borough.)*

7. In this Act the expression "a household qualification" means as respects England and Ireland, the qualification enacted by the third section of the Representation of the People Act, 1867, and the enactments amending or affecting the same, and the said section and enactments, so far as they are consistent with this Act, shall extend to counties in England and to counties and boroughs in Ireland. *(Definition of household and lodger qualification and other franchises, and application of enactments relating thereto.)*

In the construction of the said enactments, as amended and applied to Ireland, the following dates shall be substituted for the dates therein mentioned, that is to say, the *twentieth day of July* for the fifteenth day of July, the *first day of July* for the twentieth day of July, and the *first day of January* for the fifth day of January. *(30 & 31 Vict. c. 102, s. 3; 41 & 42 Vict. c. 26, ss. 5, 7. 30 & 31 Vict. c. 102, s. 4; 41 & 42 Vict. c. 26, ss. 5, 6, 7.)*

The expression "a lodger qualification" means the qualification enacted, as respects England, by the fourth section of the Representation of the People Act, 1867, and the enactments amending or affecting the same, and as respects Ireland, by the *(31 & 32 Vict. c. 49, s. 4.)*

fourth section of the Representation of the People (Ireland) Act, 1868, and the enactments amending or affecting the same, and the said section of the English Act of 1867, and the enactments amending or affecting the same, shall, so far as they are consistent with this Act, extend to counties in England, and the said section of the Irish Act of 1868, and the enactments amending or affecting the same, shall, so far as they are consistent with this Act, extend to counties in Ireland, and sections

41 & 42 Vict. c. 26, ss. 5, 6, 22.

five and six and twenty-two of the Parliamentary and Municipal Registration Act, 1878, so far as they relate to lodgings, shall apply to Ireland, and for the purpose of such application the reference in the said section six to the Representation of the People Act, 1867, shall be deemed to be made to the Representation of the People (Ireland) Act, 1868.

The expression "a household qualification" means, as respects Scotland, the qualification enacted by the third section of the Representation of the People (Scotland) Act, 1868, and the enact-

31 & 32 Vict. c. 48, s. 3.

ments amending or affecting the same, and the said section and enactments shall, so far as they are consistent with this Act, extend to counties in Scotland, and for the purpose of the said section and enactments the expression "dwelling-house" in Scotland means any house or part of a house occupied as a separate dwelling, and this definition of a dwelling-house shall be substituted for the definition contained in section fifty-nine of the

31 & 32 Vict. c. 48, s. 59.

Representation of the People (Scotland) Act, 1868.

The expression "a lodger qualification" means,

31 & 32 Vict. c. 48, s. 4.

as respects Scotland, the qualification enacted by

the fourth section of the Representation of the People (Scotland) Act, 1868, and the enactments amending or affecting the same and the said section and enactments, so far as they are consistent with this Act, shall extend to counties in Scotland.

The expression "county occupation franchise" means, as respects England, the franchise enacted by the sixth section of the Representation of the People Act, 1867; and, as respects Scotland, the 30 & 31 Vict. c. 102, s. 6. franchise enacted by the sixth section of the Representation of the People (Scotland) Act, 1868; and, 31 & 32 Vict. c. 48, s. 6. as respects Ireland, the franchise enacted by the first section of the Act of the session of the thirteenth and fourteenth years of the reign of her 13 & 14 Vict. c. 69, s. 1. present Majesty, chapter sixty-nine.

The expression "borough occupation franchise" means, as respects England, the franchise enacted by the twenty-seventh section of the Act of the session of the second and third years of the reign of King William the Fourth, chapter forty-five; and, 2 & 3 Will. 4, c. 45, s. 27. as respects Scotland, the franchise enacted by the eleventh section of the Act of the session of the second and third years of the reign of King William the Fourth, chapter sixty-five; and, as respects 2 & 3 Will. 4, c. 65, s. 11. Ireland, the franchise enacted by section five of the Act of the session of the thirteenth and fourteenth years of the reign of her present Majesty, chapter 13 & 14 Vict. c. 69, s. 5. sixty-nine, and the third section of the Representation of the People (Ireland) Act, 1868. 31 & 32 Vict. c. 49, s. 3.

Any enactments amending or relating to the county occupation franchise or borough occupation franchise other than the sections in this Act in that behalf mentioned shall be deemed to be referred to in the definition of the county occupation franchise and the borough occupation franchise in this Act mentioned.

Definition of "Representation of the People Acts" and "Registration Acts." 8. In this Act the expression " the Representation of the People Acts " means the enactments for the time being in force in England, Scotland, and Ireland respectively relating to the representation of the people, inclusive of the Registration Acts as defined by this Act.

The expression " the Registration Acts " means the enactments for the time being in force in England, Scotland, and Ireland respectively, relating to the registration of persons entitled to vote at elections for counties and boroughs, inclusive of the Rating Acts as defined by this Act.

The expressions " the Representation of the People Acts " and "the Registration Acts " respectively, where used in this Act, shall be read distributively in reference to the three parts of the United Kingdom as meaning in the case of each part the enactments for the time being in force in that part.

All enactments of the Registration Acts which relate to the registration of persons entitled to vote in boroughs in England and Scotland in respect of a household or a lodger qualification, and in boroughs in Ireland in respect of a lodger qualification, shall, with the necessary variations and alterations of precepts, notices, lists, and other forms, extend to counties as well as to boroughs.

All enactments of the Registration Acts which relate to the registration in counties and boroughs in Ireland of persons entitled to vote in respect of the county occupation franchise and the borough occupation franchise respectively, shall, with the necessary variations and alterations of precepts, notices, lists, and other forms, extend respectively to the registration in counties and boroughs in Ireland of persons entitled to vote in respect of the household qualification conferred by this Act.

9. In this Act the expression "the Rating Acts" means the enactments for the time being in force in England, Scotland, and Ireland respectively, relating to the placing of the names of occupiers on the rate book, or other enactments relating to rating in so far as they are auxiliary to or deal with the registration of persons entitled to vote at elections; and the expression "the Rating Acts" where used in this Act shall be read distributively in reference to the three parts of the United Kingdom as meaning in the case of each part the Acts for the time being in force in that part. *Definition and application of Rating Acts.*

In Scotland section fifteen of the Representation of the People (Scotland) Act, 1868, shall apply to counties as well as to burghs, and in the application thereof the word "tenant" shall include any inhabitant occupier within the meaning of this Act, and it shall be the duty of every person rated in respect of any lands and heritages which comprise any dwelling-house when applied to by the assessor to give an accurate written list of the names and designations of all men other than himself, being inhabitant occupiers of any dwelling-house forming part of such lands and heritages, and if he fail to do so he shall be liable on summary conviction to a penalty not exceeding *five pounds*, and the proviso in section two of the Act for the Valuation of Lands and Heritages in Scotland, passed in the session of the seventeenth and eighteenth years of *31 & 32 Vict. c. 48.*

the reign of Her present Majesty, chapter ninety-one, shall be repealed.

In Ireland where the owner of a dwelling-house is rated instead of the occupier, the occupier shall nevertheless be entitled to be registered as a voter, and to vote under the same conditions under which an occupier of a dwelling-house in England is entitled in pursuance of the Poor Rate Assessment and Collection Act, 1869, and the Acts amending the same, to be registered as a voter, and to vote where the owner is rated, and the enactments referred to in the First Schedule to this Act shall apply to Ireland accordingly, with the modification in that schedule mentioned.

32 & 33 Vict. c. 41.

Both in England and Ireland where a man inhabits any dwelling-house by virtue of any office, service, or employment, and is deemed for the purposes of this Act and of the Representation of the People Acts to be an inhabitant occupier of such dwelling-house as a tenant, and another person is rated or liable to be rated for such dwelling-house, the rating of such other person shall for the purposes of this Act and of the Representation of the People Acts be deemed to be that of the inhabitant occupier; and the several enactments of the Poor Rate Assessment and Collection Act, 1869, and other Acts amending the same referred to in the First Schedule to this Act shall for those purposes apply to such inhabitant occupier, and in the construction of those enactments the word "owner" shall be deemed to include a person actually rated or liable to be rated as aforesaid.

Both in England and in Ireland where a house is let out or occupied in separate parts, and any of such parts constitutes a separate dwelling-house within the meaning of the Representation of the People Acts, the overseers shall within twenty-one days after the *first of March* in every year give notice in writing to the person rated or rateable in respect of such house requiring him within fourteen days after the service of such notice to furnish in a form to be supplied by the overseers an accurate list containing the name of the occupier of every such part which constitutes a separate dwelling-house, and the person applied to shall furnish such list accordingly ; and if any overseer makes default in giving such notice as last aforesaid, or any person rated or rateable as aforesaid makes default in furnishing the list so required to be furnished by him, such overseer or person shall on summary conviction be liable to a penalty not exceeding *forty shillings.*

In any part of the United Kingdom where a man inhabits a dwelling-house in respect of which no person is rated by reason of such dwelling-house belonging to or being occupied on behalf of the Crown, or by reason of any other ground of exemption, such person shall not be disentitled to be registered as a voter, and to vote by reason only that no one is rated in respect of such dwelling-house, and that no rates are paid in respect of the same, and it shall be the duty of the persons making out the rate book or valuation roll to enter any such dwelling-house as last aforesaid in the rate book or valuation roll, together with the name of the inhabitant occupier thereof.

10. Nothing in this Act shall deprive any person- Saving. (who at the date of the passing of this Act is registered in respect of any qualification to vote for any county or borough,) of his right to be from time to time registered and to vote for such county or borough in respect of such qualification in like manner as if this Act had not passed.

Provided that where a man is so registered in respect of the county or borough occupation franchise by virtue of a qualification which also qualifies him for the franchise under this Act, he shall be entitled to be registered in respect of such latter franchise only.

Nothing in this Act shall confer on any man who is subject to any legal incapacity to be registered as a voter or to vote, any right to be registered as a voter or to vote.

Construction of Act. **11.** This Act, so far as may be consistently with the tenor thereof, shall be construed as one with the Representation of the People Acts as defined by this Act ; and the expressions " election," " county," and " borough," and other expressions in this Act and in the enactments applied by this Act, shall have the same meaning as in the said Acts.

Provided that in this Act and the said enactments—

The expression " overseers " includes assessors, guardians, clerks of unions, or other persons by whatever name known, who perform duties in relation to rating or to the registration of voters similar to those performed in relation to such matters by overseers in England.

The expression " rentcharge " includes a fee farm rent, a feu duty in Scotland, a rent seck, a chief rent, a rent of assize, and any rent or annuity granted out of land.

The expression "land or tenement" includes any part of a house separately occupied for the purpose of any trade, business or profession, and that expression and also the expression "hereditament," when used in this Act, in Scotland includes "lands and heritages."

The expression "clear yearly value" as applied to any land or tenement means in Scotland the annual value as appearing in the valuation roll, and in Ireland the net annual value at which the occupier of such land or tenement was rated under the last rate for the time being, under the Act of the session of the first and second years of the reign of Her present Majesty, chapter fifty-six, or any Acts amending the same.

12. Whereas the franchises conferred by this Act are in substitution for the franchises conferred by the enactments mentioned in the first and second parts of the second schedule hereto, be it enacted that the Acts mentioned in the first part of the said second schedule shall be repealed to the extent in the third column of that part of the said schedule mentioned except in so far as relates to the rights of persons saved by this Act ; and the Acts mentioned in the second part of the said second schedule shall be repealed to the extent in the third column of that part of the said schedule mentioned except in so far as relates to the rights of persons saved by this Act and except in so far as the enactments so repealed contain conditions made applicable by this Act to any franchise enacted by this Act.

Repeal of certain superseded sections.

FIRST SCHEDULE.

ENACTMENTS APPLIED TO IRELAND.

Session and Chapter.	Title.	Enactments Applied.
32 & 33 Vict. c. 41	The Poor Rate Assessment and Collection Act, 1869.	Section seven; section eight; section nine; section ten, and the enactment of the Representation of the People Act, 1867, therein referred to; section nineteen; section twenty, so far as regards the definition of the word "owner."
41 & 42 Vict. c. 26	The Parliamentary and Municipal Registration Act, 1878	Section fourteen.
42 & 43 Vict. c. 10	The Assessed Rates Act, 1879.	The whole Act.

MODIFICATION.

Any penalty recoverable on summary conviction may be recovered in accordance with the law relating to summary convictions in Ireland.

SECOND SCHEDULE.

PART I.

Session and Chapter.	Title or Short Title.	Extent of Repeal.
2 & 3 Will. 4, c. 45	An Act to amend the Representation of the People in England and Wales.	Section twenty, the words "or who "shall occupy as "tenant any lands "or tenements for "which he shall be "bonâ fide liable "to a yearly rent "of not less than "fifty pounds."
2 & 3 Will. 4, c. 65	An Act to amend the Representation of the People in Scotland.	Section nine, the words "or where "such tenant shall, "for the foresaid "period of twelve "months, have "been in the actual "personal occu- "pancy of any "such subject, "where the yearly "rent is not less "than fifty pounds, "or where the te- "nant, whatever "the rent may "be, has truly "paid for his in- "terest in such "subject a price, "grassum, or "consideration of "not less than "three hundred "pounds."

PART II.

Session and Chapter.	Title or Short Title.	Extent of Repeal.
2 & 3 Will. 4, c. 45	An Act to amend the Representation of the People in England & Wales.	Section twenty-seven.
2 & 3 Will. 4, c. 65	An Act to amend the Representation of the People in Scotland.	Section eleven, from the beginning of the section to the words "sixth day of April then next preceding" inclusive.
13 & 14 Vict. c. 69	An Act to amend the Laws which regulate the Qualification and Registration of Parliamentary Voters in Ireland, and to alter the Law for rating Immediate Lessors of Premises to the Poor Rate in certain Boroughs.	Sections one and five.
30 & 31 Vict. c. 102	The Representation of the People Act, 1867.	Section six.
31 & 32 Vict. c. 48	The Representation of the People (Scotland) Act, 1868.	Section six.
31 & 32 Vict. c. 49	The Representation of the People (Ireland) Act, 1868.	Section three.

INDEX.

BRADBURY, AGNEW, & CO., PRINTERS, WHITEFRIARS.